EXPATLAND

JOHN MARCARIAN

First published 2015

Expatland™
By John Marcarian
BEc, CA, M Int. Tax (Hons), FTIA, ACIS JP

Head Office:
CST Tax Advisors Pte Limited
Level 17
96 Robinson Road
SINGAPORE 068899

Editor: Carol D'Costa, Em & En Word Craft
www.caroldcosta.com

Production by

Longueville Media Pty Ltd
PO Box 205
Haberfield NSW 2045 Australia
www.longmedia.com.au
info@longmedia.com.au
Tel. +61 2 9362 8441

ISBN: 978-0-9942691-2-6
For the National Library of Australia Cataloguing-in-Publication entry please visit www.nla.gov.au

Dedication

This book is dedicated to the great many people who played a part in providing the technical and commercial experience necessary to write a book such as this.

My work experience began when I was 19 in the offices of Arthur Young (now Ernst & Young) Chatswood, Sydney, Australia.

My early mentors, Geoff Penrose and Ray Gould, at Arthur Young, Peter Allsop and Venn O'Neill from Duesburys (now Deloittes) taught me a great deal about the business of being a chartered accountant.

Once I commenced practice, Joe Bongiorno was a great mentor. He helped me develop my understanding of the rules of the business world and how to assist clients. I appreciated Joe's guidance and I still use the lessons he taught me on a daily basis.

A special mention goes to John Lucas, for many years with the United Nations and the World Health Organization, who lit the fire of my imagination about how a chartered accountant could build an international career. Feroze Sukh has also been a major support to me over the past decade.

I am also very thankful for the support of my loving parents. My brother, Matthew Marcarian, has shown deep commitment and care for me along the way as well. My thanks to the rest of the global team at CST Tax Advisors for their help in making this book possible.

Most importantly, though, I dedicate this book to my wife, Taleen, and my two daughters, Isabelle and Natalie. Their unfailing love and support for me while I travelled the length and breadth of Expatland has been a constant source of inspiration and motivation. The journey continues …

In Memory of My Grandparents

Nefton and Annie Basil

About the author

By his mid teens John Marcarian had read his first book on international tax planning and was hooked. John has since become a chartered accountant, international tax advisor and the founder of the global business CST Tax Advisors.

Throughout his youth John developed a keen interest in business, sport and travel. At the age of 25, although a tax manager with Deloitte, he recognised that starting his own business was the direction his professional career was headed.

In 1992 John founded what is now CST Tax Advisors, and in 2004 he established its Singapore office. Since that time, CST Tax Advisors has spread to many global locations. The company remains the only business that focuses solely on the tax needs of global expats living throughout Expatland.

A regular speaker, John travels widely, presenting numerous technical and business papers around the globe to organisations such as the American Australian Association, AustCham Singapore, Israel-Asia Chamber of Commerce, and Australian Business (in London) to name a few. He has also assisted clients in more than 50 countries.

John is married with two daughters. In his spare time he is learning Brazilian Portuguese and surfing.

Contents

Disclaimer

Foreword

When John Marcarian asked me to write the Foreword to his book *Expatland*, I was struck by a couple of initial thoughts.

The first thought was that although there is an elegant simplicity, which the word Expatland captures very well, the 'country' itself is geographically diverse and its inhabitants can be from all walks of life.

Indeed, Expatland inhabitants can be, as was my case for many years, a sports professional living overseas while plying their trade, a global executive working for a multinational or an international businessperson living and working away from home.

From personal experience I have seen a significant rise in the number of Australians and other nationalities moving internationally to live and work.

The world is a much more interconnected place now than it was when I first represented Australia in 1970. In those days the term 'expat' was virtually unheard of. Today, however, people are moving overseas to live and work with far greater frequency.

The second thought that occurred to me was that I could really have done with John's book much earlier!

Together with my wife, Judy, we have been expats in many locations and we encountered a number of the challenges that John discusses with such clarity in *Expatland*.

We eventually solved these challenges, but having this book earlier would have made the process of overcoming them much more straightforward.

In my time as a professional cricketer, Captain of the Australian Cricket Team and as an international cricket coach, my approach has always been to plan carefully before any significant undertaking.

To my mind John has done a terrific job of covering most of the things that a future inhabitant of Expatland needs to consider and plan for.

The book is full of very insightful observations, suggestions and ideas for action.

I believe this book is a must read for anyone heading to Expatland.

Enjoy the journey.

Greg Chappell, MBE
Australian Cricket Captain (1975–1983)
International Cricket Coach

Introduction

Welcome to Expatland

Expatland is the name I have given to the 'special country' where global expats live! The aim of my book *Expatland* is to help you learn about a variety of subjects that you will need to know before you move to Expatland, whether it is to Europe, Asia Pacific, the US or elsewhere. The book cover illustrates how I imagine Expatland might look like.

It is not my intent to be prescriptive in the sense of which particular countries are addressed, because the reality is that Expatland can be comprised of every country in the world.

The background to *Expatland* started when my firm CST Tax Advisors began in 1992. I soon noticed that a gap existed in the market with respect to helping private individual expatriates co-ordinate and manage their tax accounting and legal affairs across international markets. After a number of years dealing with global expatriate clients, I decided that a book about Expatland would be very helpful to future residents planning their move.

My hope is that my book will be a valuable guide to help you make the big move and will provide you with things to think about; points to follow up; facts to learn; and steps to take.

1

THE MOVE TO EXPATLAND

The opportunity for overseas employment appeals to many people and attracts significant interest across the globe. If your objective is to enrich your own life and your family's with a range of cultural experiences, then relocating to Expatland may make good sense.

You may be moving to Expatland as part of your current employment or to pursue new opportunities. If you are moving with an existing employer, the motivation for this may be to demonstrate support to senior global management or to gain experience and advance within the corporation. Other expats may view life in Expatland as a way to travel to foreign countries and learn about new cultures and gain fresh experiences.

Regardless of your personal motivation, there are a number of important planning points to consider and resolve.

Often expats arrive in Expatland without a detailed understanding of the cost of living. It is worth noting that a higher salary may in fact be offset by a higher cost of living in Expatland.

For example, some costs, such as education, may be much higher than in your home country. If you are moving to a lower cost city in Expatland, then it may be that moving country while still

on the same level of salary you have already could still provide a significant economic advantage.

This may be due to the fact that you are able to rent out your family home and reduce your mortgage faster than if you resided there. The position has to be considered, as do other financial planning opportunities, which are discussed further. Money as a reason to move to Expatland is just one consideration.

Our experience is that life in Expatland is not for everyone. It can present its own unique challenges, and therefore it is beneficial, wherever possible, to keep close connections with former employers and work associates. That way, if you decide to return to your home country, you will be kept abreast of work and other opportunities that may come up after your departure.

Equally important is that you maintain your knowledge of any technical and business developments in your area of work that occur while you are in Expatland. The reason for this is that your knowledge may have been current when you left your homeland, but without maintaining that knowledge you face the prospect of becoming outdated. This makes it harder to return if you wish to stay in the same industry.

It may be equally likely that destination Expatland offers you a greater range of training and experience that will provide better opportunities on your return to your home country than if you had not left in the first place.

An important question for a number of families is whether the whole family should travel to Expatland to begin with.

It is commonly the case that the man of the household has his job relocated, but it does work both ways. Sometimes the female spouse or partner may, for a variety of reasons, not be able to join the expat overseas. It may be that her occupation offers limited potential in Expatland.

Often referred to as the 'trailing spouse', the male or female life partner will need to evaluate their journey to Expatland from both financial and non-financial perspectives.

We have seen many cases of such spouses or partners leaving good positions in their home country but not being able to secure employment in Expatland for some time. This can cause marital unrest and should be considered carefully.

There are exceptions to a lack of mobility – for example, EU nationals can usually enter other EU countries looking for employment, and some countries such as Australia and New Zealand also offer relaxed entry rules.

As a general rule, a trailing spouse will have a higher likelihood of employment if they possess specialist or professional qualifications and experience. This will clearly be so for those professions that are in high demand in Expatland, such as medical, dental, IT, and engineering professionals. In some countries foreign language teachers are highly sought after.

At a minimum, it is important to confirm if their present qualifications are sufficient to gain employment in Expatland. Your spouse or partner may be required to obtain upgraded or new qualifications prior to beginning work.

General Information on Expatland

'Expatland' is a 'country' with more than 230 million people in a place consisting of different nationalities from all over the world. If it were a single country, it would be the fifth largest country in the world after China, India, US, Indonesia and Brazil.

During the time I have been an expatriate, I have discovered that life in Expatland is a constant series of new discoveries.

Many global expatriates move to a variety of locations over a number of years and the challenges that arise when moving from jurisdiction to jurisdiction are significant.

Some of these challenges will include finding a support network in the country of arrival; getting out, exploring and understanding the difference between the countries; figuring out how to stay in touch with family and friends; and perhaps the most significant from our perspective and the focus of this book are the accounting, taxation, legal, financial planning and insurance issues associated with moving to Expatland. (Appendix A, 'Special Terms', covers some key terminology you may find helpful.)

Throughout the book we will cover topics related to planning for life in Expatland, particularly in the above areas. We will also touch on most commonly asked questions about life as an expatriate in Appendix B, 'Expat Views from Expatland'.

Overall, the aim of the book is to form a basis for the reader to consider strategies and their approach to adapting, living, surviving, but most importantly *thriving* in Expatland.

Here are a few interesting statistics about Expatland to think about:

Australian Expats

Approximately more than 1 million Australian citizens or 5 per cent of the population live outside Australia in more than 20 other countries. The majority, 48 per cent, are based in Europe and the US, with approximately 24 per cent living in Asia.

While New Zealand, the UK and the US remain the most popular countries for departing Aussies, the focus is shifting towards our Asian neighbours. Hong Kong is a stronghold for Australians looking to do business in Asia and there has been a notable increase in emigration to China, Japan, Singapore and Thailand.

Australian-born emigration still occurs in greatest numbers to the UK, the US and to New Zealand. The next most popular destinations in 2010/11 were Singapore (9.4 per cent), Hong Kong (5.8 per cent) and the United Arab Emirates (5.2 per cent).

Foreign-born residents have made up approximately half of all Australian permanent departures since 1998/99 with the largest groups originating from New Zealand, the UK, China, Hong Kong (SARS) and Vietnam. Most of these individuals called Australia home for five years or more and then left to return to their country of birth.

The diagram on the following page gives a more extensive breakdown of the Australian expatriate diaspora.

Regions with significant populations

Australian diaspora in excess of 1,000,000

UK	280,000
US	200,000
Greece	100,000
Hong Kong	90,000
New Zealand	70,000
Canada	35,000
Italy	30,000
Lebanon	25,000
Vietnam	22,000
Singapore	20,000
Thailand	20,000
UAE	16,000
China	15,000
Germany	15,000
Netherlands	15,000

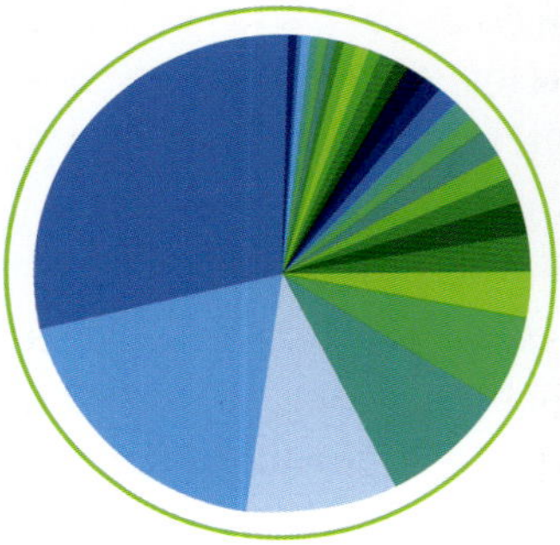

PNG	15,000
Turkey	12,000
Indonesia	12,000
Japan	11,000
Ireland	10,000
South Africa	8,000
Israel	7,000
South Korea	7,000
Taiwan	7,000
Philippines	6,000
France	5,500
Saudi Arabia	5,000
Switzerland	5,000
Cambodia	3,000

Sources:
http://advance.org/australians-abroad-preliminary-findings-on-the-australian-diaspora/
http://en.wikipedia.org/wiki/Australian_diaspora

German, Dutch & French Expats

The following statistics reflect the flow of some European expatriates:

- There are more than 3 million Germans living abroad. For example, in Atlanta, Georgia, there is a community of 50,000 German expats.
- More than 1 million French expats work outside France – 20,000 live and work in Hong Kong.
- There are more than 500,000 Dutch expats living and working abroad, with many based in Hong Kong, Singapore and Indonesia.

Source: Based on the publication Trends in International Migration 2004 – http://www.oecd.org/migration/mig/TIM%202004%20chapter%202.pdf

British Expats

Almost 5 million British expats are now living and working abroad, helping to shape the communities they live in. The top three most popular destinations for British expats are Australia, Spain and the US, according to the fifth annual NatWest International Personal Banking Quality of Life Index.*

The global NatWest IPB Quality of Life report, in conjunction with the Centre of Future Studies, reveals that overall, 41 countries each have a British expat population of at least 10,000 and 112 countries have at least 1000.

* All data sourced by the Centre for Future Studies.
Source: http://britishexpats.com/news/latest-news/expats-world-hands/

US Expats

According to unofficial estimates from the US Department of State (late 2011), 6.32 million Americans, excluding the military, live in 160 plus countries. In fact, if all these Americans were placed in one state, it would be the 17th most populous state in the US.

However, because Americans residing outside the US are not counted in the US consensus, this estimate, as all 'counts' of Americans abroad, is based on a limited amount of date combined with intelligent guesswork.

The following diagram shows estimated figures by region:

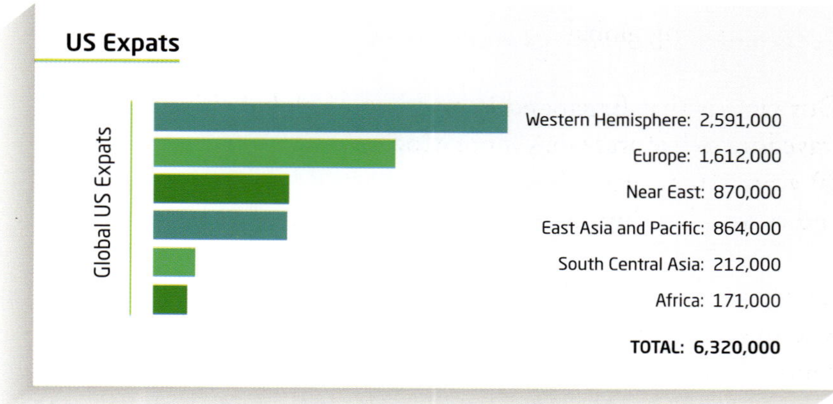

Source: http://www.aaro.org/about-aaro/6m-americans-abroad

In addition

- 85 per cent of more than 1 million expatriates in China work for international firms.

- In the past two years alone, the number of Spanish expatriates in Brazil has more than doubled.

- The Middle East and North Africa are popular with younger expatriates.

- 67 per cent in Qatar and 67 per cent in Bahrain (of expatriates) have higher incomes compared with 52 per cent globally.

- Vietnam, Indonesia and Mexico are fast-growing markets in attracting global expatriates.

Our view is that Expatland is made up of global citizens who are travelling to live and work more widely than at any time in the past 50 years. This means the need for cross-border taxation, and legal and estate planning along with accounting services is essential.

On a global basis, CST Tax Advisors services clients in Expatland, who in our view often struggle to be looked after globally by single country accounting and tax firms. Typically accounting firms have been built on reputation and years of providing services to a core group of customers. Market forces have begun to erode this 'one firm' business model. Hence when expats move to Expatland, often their domestic tax advisors need help to ensure their clients are looked after properly.

Understanding Cultural Differences

Before you arrive in Expatland, it is important to do some research on common customs and practices that will greet you. Learning all you can before you begin work in Expatland is a must. Keep in mind that these cultural issues will cover most aspects of your daily life.

Cultural practices obviously differ depending upon where you live in Expatland. For example, social drinking, which may be completely acceptable in your home country, may not be permitted in your Expatland – or a simple expression of distaste for a 'moon cake' during a festival in Singapore may alienate you from local co-workers.

Some years ago while I was travelling to Kuala Lumpur, Malaysia, I was invited to dinner with some clients and their local partners. All was going well until the highly 'aromatic' fruit durian was served up for dessert. For those of you that have not had the fruit, its taste and aroma is hard to describe. Out of politeness I did not refuse the dessert at first, but after displaying an initial liking for it I realised by the third helping that I had eaten more than enough.

As we will discuss, along with being sensitive to cultural nuances, you need to take particular care in understanding the terms and conditions of your employment agreement. You should carefully review your contract to determine what these employment obligations and entitlements are.

Your Expatland city may have detailed laws covering many aspects of employment including working hours, remuneration, overtime and other pay entitlements. If these are not clearly stated in your employment agreement before you move, then changing or negotiating when you are there could create unnecessary problems.

In some Expatland cities you may be required to join a union, while in others you will have the right to choose whether you do or not. It is best to understand what the cost benefit is of joining a union or association versus not joining. Also make sure you understand how many public holidays exist, as this can impact your earnings if you work on a commission basis.

The working week may vary for religious and historical reasons, and therefore you could be working from Saturday to Wednesday, which would be the case in Saudi Arabia, or going to the office on Sunday, which is what you would do in Israel.

The hours of work are often different in Expatland as well. In some Asian countries, it is common practice for employees to remain at work well into the evening – workers will often stay until their superior has left for the night. However, this is not usually the case for employees from western countries.

The long hours may not necessarily mean that employees are more productive, however. In fact, the same work may just be spread over a longer period. Nonetheless, you should be prepared to adapt to working the local time system or otherwise expect to stand out.

Also note that the new organisation may have a different company culture than that in your home country. This may exhibit itself in the requirements for work attire and the conduct of meetings. For those in management, understanding the local culture is crucial because you may need to exhibit more flexibility when managing local employees.

Expatland Culture is the Way You See It

Many expats unwittingly break some cultural taboos upon arrival in Expatland, even if they move to a part of Expatland similar to their home country. An example can be speaking about personal finances and asking questions of people from a local culture. This may be normal behaviour in your home country, but it may be far from acceptable in Expatland.

In case of a secondment to an Islamic country, it is worth noting that Muslims have particular dietary customs that may differ from yours. For example, Muslims do not eat pork or drink alcohol, and they generally only consume food prepared in the method prescribed by Islamic law. This is referred to as 'halal'.

During the month of Ramadan, Muslims fast during daylight hours. Hence it is probably going to be seen as insensitive if you eat in front of Muslim friends or co-workers during the day.

In other Asian parts of Expatland, such as China, there is a concept known as *guanxi*, which is very important in both social and business interactions. It refers to a relationship established over time in which favours are owed and mutual obligations are due between certain parties.

The concept of respect is also of major importance in China. Showing respect for elders, visitors and those that you have a *guanxi* relationship with is paramount. This type of respect manifests itself in seemingly excessive politeness.

It is vital that you do not cause a client, friend or co-worker in China to lose face. This can irreparably damage a relationship. Also for expats moving to India it is worth noting that the left hand is considered an 'unclean' hand by many and hence giving or receiving anything with your left hand is considered uncultured.

These are just some examples of cultural differences, but indeed research into the part of Expatland where you are travelling to is very important.

Expatland Arrivals

Before you leave for Expatland, it is important to have a plan in place well before you arrive. Consider some of the following points pre-arrival:

- Confirm if you are required to register with the immigration authorities.

- Always register with your own country's consulate when you arrive in Expatland and make sure that you have your home country consulate details readily at hand.

- In the event that there is some type of national emergency, the consulate will be an important contact point for you.

- Review and check out mobile phone plans so you can change from your home country mobile phone as quickly as possible.

- Review and check out Internet plans and the requirements, ID and other essentials needed to set up an account. In some parts of Expatland, in the absence of a tax identification number you will be unable to sign up for certain communication services.

- Set up a mail redirection in your home country to another address in your home country rather than an international redirection. Not only is this usually a less expensive option, but it also lessens the likelihood of mail getting lost internationally.

- Research how reliable postal deliveries are in your new country, and use special mail or courier services if necessary.

- When you arrive, remember to let your friends and family know you are safe and give them your new address details. Often this is overlooked during the settling in process.

- Keeping in touch with your home country friends also covers the possibility that your time in Expatland may be shorter than you think and hence you may be home sooner than you think.

- When you arrive in Expatland try to make friends and get to know work colleagues as soon as possible. There is much to be gained from forming a social circle to support you and your family in Expatland.

- In some parts of Expatland it is more difficult to make friends with locals. Care must be taken to understand the local culture prior to the process of beginning to make friends.

- Generally speaking, you will find locals in Expatland friendly and welcoming if you adapt to their culture.

- Consider joining clubs in Expatland that offer you the possibility of continuing pursuits you followed back in your home country.

- Depending upon your location in Expatland, making friends with local councillors or other people of influence will assist you and your family to become known and accepted.

- It is worth remembering that the months of good work in building relationships in the local community can be undone with a quip or otherwise harmless remark in Expatland. Locals may have a completely different way of looking at things.

- Expat clubs are often a great way of making friends upon arrival. These clubs are generally filled with expats who have gone through similar changes to you, so they can be a good source of knowledge about transitional issues.

Mental Health

Given the significance of the change, it is not unusual for there to be stress with the huge transition the family is going through.

Much of this is normal and manageable. However, if the issues are more serious and feelings of negativity and depression begin to occur, then it is essential to seek out professional assistance.

AT A GLANCE

- Have your plans for employment, accommodation and schools well in place before you embark on your journey.
- Research as much as possible about the culture and main religion of the country you are moving to.
- Make friends in Expatland as soon as possible; this will normalise the new situation for you and your family.
- Examine the terms and conditions of your employment contract scrutinisingly before signing.
- Register with your local consulate when you arrive in Expatland.
- Keep in contact with friends and colleagues back home.
- Don't forget to keep abreast with changes to your industry or career sector occurring in your homeland.
- Watch for signs of stress in your family. If the issues are significant, such as depression or feelings of negativity, then seek professional assistance.
- Don't expect that your spouse will easily find employment in the new country. If employment for your spouse is not an option, think how this will affect your family finances.
- Your new company may not have the same work culture or work ethic that you are accustomed to. You may have to work on weekends or later in the night.
- Don't break cultural or religious taboos. This can be serious, depending on which Expatland you are moving to.

2

EXPATLAND FAMILY LIFE

Childcare

The cost of childcare in Expatland has to be considered if both expats want to work. The other major issue is a non-financial one – it's about the quality and availability of childcare centres and trained staff.

From our experience, we see that many expats in Asia opt for live-in home help to manage the home and care for the children while the parents work.

In Singapore, for example, most of the maids are from the Philippines. While experience suggests they are caring individuals often having done multiple postings, it is worth remembering that these 'nannies' may have limited education and communication skills.

Hence many expats in Expatland ensure that their young children have access to trained professionals in their early years ahead of what might be the case in their home country.

It is essential that if live-in help is to be deployed, the individual should be recruited through a reliable, well-known service. These agencies usually perform sufficient background checks and they only place reliable people.

In most cases the expat will have to sponsor the nanny into the country and pay for all related costs, such as healthcare and check-ups.

Your Partner

For the non-working spouse who joins the working partner, there can be many benefits indeed, especially concerning the children.

It may be that the now non-working spouse does not need a full-time nanny or maid but rather can enjoy the opportunity to spend more time with her children. In other cases, the spouse can use the time for study, hobbies or charity work. (Charity work is a terrific way of meeting the locals in Expatland.)

Feedback from many clients over the years is that the non-working spouse (I much prefer this term than 'trailing spouse') can feel isolated. This is particularly likely to be the case if, apart from cultural differences in Expatland, the non-working spouse does not develop a local support network. This marginalisation is further exacerbated by the absence of family or friends.

Therefore, it is very important to make a determined effort early on to develop a social plan. Initiating contact with other new arrivals through chambers of commerce or expat groups is a tried and true approach for many people.

The Family

Before the move, ask your children – especially the older ones – for their feedback on the move to Expatland and what they think would be new experiences they could achieve after the move.

It is not easy moving your entire household to Expatland, so having all the family onboard is a must. A post-arrival plan for each family member is a great way of engaging everyone in the relocation.

Family life in Expatland is often something that changes family dynamics and established patterns of family behaviour that may have been normal in your home country.

Although a move to Expatland is in many cases work related, feedback from expats we act for suggests it is also a tremendous opportunity to develop family life in new ways and pursue new options for advancement.

Also equally well known is the fact that Expatland can have a significant impact on children. Many of them become what sociologist and anthropologist Dr Ruth Hill Useem termed in the 1960s as '*Third Culture Kids*' (TCK). TCK has been described as "a person who has spent a significant part of his or her developmental years outside the parents' culture".

"The TCK frequently builds relationships to all of the cultures, while not having full ownership in any. Although elements from each culture may be assimilated into the TCK's life experience, the sense of belonging is in relationship to others of similar background." Source: **http://www.tckworld.com/useem/home.html**

It is not the purpose of this chapter to address TCKs in depth, but it is worth including some of the following observations on family life from our clients during and after their time in Expatland.

1. The role of the family is of central importance in assisting your child to adapt to life in Expatland. If possible, try to spend as much time with your children as you can while they are adjusting to life in Expatland.

2. Involve your children as much as possible in the journey. For example, help them learn about the history of their forthcoming new home in Expatland and its culture in the lead up to the move.

3. For younger children, make sure they take their favourite toys or pets that can be of comfort to them when leaving their home.

4. Ensure that your children regularly keep in touch with their own circle of friends in your home country.

5. It can help if they develop a new skill (maybe a sport, music or a hobby) to take with them to Expatland as this will broaden the potential circle of friends and ability to bond with new children in Expatland.

6. Assist them in making new friends outside of school in Expatland by undertaking extra school activities wherever possible.

7. As they will make friends with children who will leave Expatland and move back to their home country, think about establishing a map showing where they have moved to and then helping your child learn about those countries.

8. For most of the expats who provided feedback to us, the benefits of life as an expat kid with new experiences and new friendships are worth the ups and downs of the transition.

9. Take opportunities to do things as a family that you would not do back home. Memories are made out of doing new things and experiencing them together.

10. Help your child develop resilience, as this is a quality they will need in Expatland.

11. Encouraging your kids to try new things and develop new skills means that failure will be part of the journey. Make it clear to them that not succeeding first time is fine.

12. Learning the language of their Expatland helps them adapt.

13. Remember that a cohesive family is the foundation upon which a child's world is built. Even if one parent is travelling significantly in and out of Expatland for work reasons, emotional support and keeping in touch can help the child adjust.

14. Use technology to stay connected with your child if you travel for work. Skype and other forms of keeping in touch such as WhatsApp, FaceTime and Viber help a child know they are important.

15. Bringing back gifts from places you travel helps fire their imagination and gives them some perspective of your world.

16. If they have special learning needs, then make sure those needs are able to be met in Expatland.

17. Whatever their outlet – sport, dance or music – ensure that they can continue their hobbies and develop new ones.

18. Where possible keeping to some form of routine and structure even with a spouse who has to travel a lot in Expatland provides regularity to your child. This sense of

routine gives a child certainty and control over some aspect of the family schedule.

19. In terms of childcare, make sure you understand the qualification process required to be undertaken in Expatland as it may differ significantly from your home country.

20. Consider setting some family objectives in Expatland for all the family to focus on doing together. By setting out realistic family objectives you put in place a tangible list of the benefits of moving to Expatland.

21. Identify whether you plan your move to be a short-term or a long-term one. Consider some broader questions – for example, do you wish to obtain permanent residency in Expatland or opt for dual nationality. Knowing the broad plan can help the family understand your long-term goals and objectives.

22. If time allows, consider doing new things to improve your health such as meditation, more exercise and/or other relaxation pursuits. Investing in more 'me' time is a good way to adapt to the journey.

In Conclusion

While these initial observations about moving to Expatland may seem to be confronting, like most things in life recognising the issues is the best way of dealing with them.

We have worked with many clients over the years, and by far those who have gained the most out of the journey to Expatland have considered all the key issues outlined in this book, not only financial and legal but also cultural and lifestyle.

We are sure that some other issues not covered here will present themselves. However, by staying alert and responsive to change those issues can also be addressed.

AT A GLANCE

- Childcare issues are not just about the cost. It is important that home help is recruited through an agency and screened judiciously.
- A non-working spouse may not need full-time help, choosing instead to take the opportunity to spend more time with the children.
- With home help, it's a good idea that the non-working spouse uses the spare time for study, hobbies or charity work. This way they will feel more integrated with their new life in Expatland.
- Before your move to Expatland, ask your children, especially if they are older, for feedback on the move to Expatland and what they think would be new experiences they could achieve after the move.
- Pre-arrival, involve your children as much as possible. Help them learn about the history of their destination, for example. A post-arrival plan for each family member is a great way of engaging everyone in the relocation.
- The transition to life in Expatland can be difficult, so try to spend as much time with your children as you can while they are adjusting to their new life.
- Let your younger children take their favourite toys or pets (if viable).
- If you have to travel away from home in Expatland, keep in regular touch with your children by using technology such as Skype, WhatsApp or Viber.

- Keep a sound routine for the children. This regularity gives a child certainty and control over some aspect of the family schedule.
- Set some family objectives in Expatland for all the family to focus on doing together.
- Identify whether you plan your move to be a short-term or a long-term one. Knowing the broad plan can help the family understand your long-term goals and objectives.

3

EXPATLAND EDUCATION

Planning your children's education is one of the most important tasks a parent can face, and in Expatland the range of schools will most likely be many and varied. Where possible, discuss with your children in advance about the change in their educational environment.

Naturally enough, changing country and schools may cause some excitement and anxiety in your children, so making them part of the decision is important. This is part of the feedback many of our expat clients provided.

Some of the FAQs in Appendix B, 'Expat Views from Expatland', reflect the variety of observations to finding schools in Expatland.

However, broadly speaking, feedback I have received from expats is that children should:

- Prepare To-Do lists to help them prepare for school.

- Find out about the activities at the school, including extra-curricular choices.

- Understand what subjects are going to be taught at their new school.

- Work out what they would like to take to school with them. Parents should first check if mobile phones or other electronic devices are allowed at the school.

- Email or contact grandparents and friends back in the home country with information about their new school.

The following section discusses other points to help your children settle into their new educational environment.

Various Education Systems

In different parts of Expatland, there are varying commencement ages for education. In some countries it is four or five years of age, but in many European countries, it is six years.

Often expats seek out primary schools that offer an education program based on their home country or look for teachers who are from their home country. This has benefits and can make a return to the education system of your home country easier when the time comes to leave Expatland.

When it comes to secondary schooling, the decision is a serious one. To make this even more complex, there are significant differences between the educational systems in different parts of Expatland. Similar to the thoughts around which primary schools to choose, you will need to consider which secondary school will allow the smoother transition back to a school in the home country if you are planning on heading back before the children have completed their education.

In some parts of Expatland, students are split into different types of schools at secondary level depending on learning ability, a teacher's recommendation and/or parental preferences.

In some cities in Expatland the education system will offer separate schools for children on the basis of sex, religion or language. For example, let us consider Saudi Arabia. It is the law to segregate children in a certain way.

The state education system in Saudi Arabia is, for the large part, weak and poorly administered when compared with that of the Western world. Furthermore, only locals and naturalised Arabs are allowed to send their children to Saudi public schools; expat children in Saudi Arabia do not have the option to enrol.

There are a number of international schools in Saudi Arabia that offer diverse curricula. Expats living in the Kingdom either choose to send their children to a private international school or opt to send them to boarding school back in their home country.

Some of the Saudi Arabian international schools are governed by embassies while others are privately organised and host multiple curricula under a single roof. It is not necessary for expat children to attend the school sponsored by their country of origin, although the logistical transition between the old and new education systems tend to be the easiest in this situation.

Unlike Saudi public schools, where boys and girls are segregated, international schools are usually co-educational. For the most part, international schools are not selective; but in some cases, embassy-run institutions do give preference to their respective nationalities as a priority. The US and UK schools both adhere to this principle.

This is clearly something to consider if you are moving to a part of Expatland that has a variety of languages and religions.

Different Varieties of Schools

The common choice for many expats is whether to send their children to international or local schools. In considering which schools to send your children, the following points will be relevant:

- Explore the different types of academic programs available.
- What are the school fees and costs of any extra-curricular activities?
- Inquire about the waiting list at the school. If there is a long waiting list, you will need to explore alternatives.
- Confirm what languages are taught at the school and which language the classes are taught in.
- What is the proximity of the school to your home.
- Find out what the culture and nationalities of the other students are.

International Schools

Most parts of Expatland have their international schools in their capital cities. The education system of these schools is generally designed for the children of expats who wish to undertake a curriculum that is accepted internationally, such as the International Baccalaureate or those that can be found in their home country.

As international schools, which usually teach in English, attract children from a wide variety of countries the education standard is fairly high and the academic results are usually very good. Their school curriculum is generally from the UK or the US.

A number of international schools also provide boarding facilities, while others are only day schools; they also offer pre-school educational programs and/or nursery facilities as part of the school. As would be expected, boarding schools fees are much higher.

These international schools are very popular options for expat families, particularly those on short-term assignments. However, most international schools charge significant fees. For those expats on a full expat package, their employer will usually fund this cost.

The fees generally increase in line with the age of the children as is common in schools in your home country.

Be aware that some schools have significant waiting lists, so if you are planning to come to Expatland you should consider the waiting period or have one or two alternative back-up schools available.

In addition to annual yearly fees, it is worth considering the other expenses that you are likely to face when sending your child to an international school.

Such expenses include extra-curricular activities, uniform, registration fees, sporting equipment and travel expenses. These costs are in addition to the basic tuition fee.

While the costs are expensive, sometimes expats have no choice, because local schooling, which may be cheaper, may not be available to expats.

On other occasions the local schools may be full and given that they are generally less expensive, demand is expected to be stronger from the local populace.

Quite reasonably you may be concerned about the potential effect on your child having to learn a new language and adapt to a new culture if your child is placed in a local school.

Every child is different, of course, and some children will take to the cultural differences in Expatland very well. Some older children may struggle as they probably have the most established friendships in their home country.

International schools provide many advantages for expatriate children, such as:

- Less interruption to their education through the use of overseas trained teaching staff

- Providing an educational structure and environment that in many cases is closer to that of their home country location

- Generally they have smaller class sizes than most local schools

- Opportunities for interaction with more international expat kids

- Usually they have more well-resourced facilities, such as swimming pools, computer centres, libraries and sporting resources.

While fees are much higher than local schools, it is common to have local students attending the school; understanding the percentage of local children attending is important. Some reasons for this are to understand how your child will fit in and be able to relate to fellow classmates in terms of language, culture and interests.

To help you choose an international school, the following 10 points will serve as a guideline:

1. Investigate all the international schools in your chosen destination.

2. Speak with other parents who have children in the school.

3. Review the Internet forums for comments on the particular international schools.

4. Ask for any data the school has on academic performance.

5. Examine the profiles and backgrounds of the teaching staff.

6. Find out what external opportunities there are for excursions or extra-curricular activities.

7. Given that most private international schools are privately run, consider what opportunities exist for you to become involved.

8. Understand the period of the waiting list and any entrance exam requirements.

9. Consider if the school has an international affiliation with a broader educational group as this will probably result in a higher level of educational standards.

10. There may also be the opportunity to study part of the time in a foreign-affiliated school if you child is pursuing an international program.

Local Schools

If you want your child to have an 'immersion' experience or for those families making a longer-term commitment to a country, it may be advantageous to enrol your child at a local school.

In the event that your child does not speak the local language, then surrounding them with native speakers will aid their adoption of the language. Language tuition after school hours can also help children adopt the local language more easily.

Forming local friendships is also easier for you and your family if the children attend a local school. However, there are some challenges in attending a local school. Some of these are as follows:

- Adjusting to a new school environment can be difficult.

- Being treated as foreigners is often a new and challenging experience.

- In the event the school has a religious program, see if it is mandatory for your child to attend.

- The attitude to homework may be significantly different than in your home country.

The requirements for children to attend the local school vary in different parts of Expatland, so I would strongly suggest that you research this before your departure to Expatland.

It is important to understand any entrance requirements for local or international schools well in advance of your arrival in Expatland.

Bilingual local schools that offer courses in, say, English as well as the local language give your children the ability to phase-in their language skills.

Boarding Schools in Your Home Country

Often one of the chief drivers for expats to return to their home country is secondary or high school education for their children.

An alternative to the whole family returning home might be to consider boarding schools either in your home country or another location.

While it is not the function of this book to examine the pros and cons of boarding school, recognising this as an option and discussing it with your spouse can be a worthwhile exercise.

If you are considering a boarding school in your home country or any other country, then finding the answers to the following questions will help in your research:

1. Is the boarding school a seven days a week boarding school?

2. How is after school and weekend time planned?

3. Does the school offer support services to assist with study, and if your children require assistance due to special needs are these addressed?

4. Does the school board have health and safety policies that your spouse/partner agree with?

5. Does the school allow the students to stay with visiting relatives from the home country on weekends or allow access for social visits?

6. How many of the students board – the majority or the minority?

7. What is the cultural mix of the children who are boarders?

8. Are your religious practices supported?

9. What medical and dental facilities exist to assist boarders?

10. What are the additional costs of boarding school, including travel to and from Expatland.

If Expatland does not provide secondary education that you consider suitable for your child, then a boarding school in your home country may be your best choice.

Funding Education in Expatland

In many cases, education in a number of well-developed parts of Expatland can be significantly expensive. Feedback from my clients reveal that many couples are caught out by how expensive education in Expatland can be. Recently one Hong Kong bound client changed their view of accepting a job offer when they calculated the cost of education in Hong Kong. Our client worked out that despite a US$200,000 increase in his base compensation – he would be US$50,000 worse off by moving!

Those expats whose home country provides good state schooling at minimal cost often struggle with the thought of paying US$25,000 or more for quality education. The expenses can be prohibitive, even at pre-school or primary school level.

We recommend that for those expats not on a full 'expat' package, the cost of education should be one of the first things planned for.

It might be that tax savings that arise in Expatland greatly exceed the cost of your child's education and the expense is therefore not a problem. However, if cost is an issue, here are some suggestions about funding your education costs:

1. Prepare a forecast of the cost of your children's education for the next five years.

2. Increase that budget for tuition costs that are not in the standard fee base.

3. Establish a line of credit against assets that can be leveraged.

4. Use the line of credit account to pay the expenses, and then set up a monthly principal and interest repayment over a 10- or 15-year period.

5. The advantage of using a debt facility against an existing asset – rather than selling the asset itself – is that by holding

the asset you have the potential to make capital gains. If you sell the asset to fund a major working expense, it eliminates the ability to make long-term capital gains.

6. Gradually increasing the loan account by drawing down for education expenses while maintaining a regular monthly payment can be a more effective way of meeting school costs that just paying from your direct salary or sale of assets.

One of my clients had never made allowances for the education funding of their first two children, and then while in Expatland they had twins! Hence long-term commitments can arise unexpectedly.

However, there is always a way of managing cash flow if enough feasibility planning goes in at an early stage. Identifying which school your children will be attending before you have left your home country is a good start to a good plan.

Tuition fees vary widely in different parts of Expatland. In the event that your employer is willing to assist you cover the cost or some of the cost of educating your children, please get that commitment in writing as soon as you can.

Also, if you are having your income ‘equalised’ to your home country, make sure that any tax benefits you get from education in your home country are factored into the negotiation about your employee compensation. Some examples of tax benefits could be rebates for each child of school age or cash grants paid by some country to parents of school age children.

Academic Scholarships

One way of reducing the cost of educating your children is to consider schools that offer scholarships. A number of schools in Expatland allow for a scholarship on a full basis or a part scholarship that covers some of the education costs.

Some schools allow an application for scholarship at the commencement of each school year. Others may only provide for one or two opportunities to gain a scholarship, so consider this aspect carefully when applying for a place in these schools.

AT A GLANCE

- It is vital that you do extensive research into the types of schooling available in Expatland well before leaving the home country.
- If your employer is not paying for the costs of your children's education, prepare a feasibility plan for funding education costs well in advance of departure.
- Wherever possible, have pre-departure discussions with your children about the change in their educational environment.
- Give the children To-Do lists to help them prepare for school. Ask them to find out as much as they can about the school they will be attending in Expatland. Transitioning to a new school in a new country can be stressful for children as well as for adults, and the more they participate in the move, the more comfortable they may feel about it.
- Choose a secondary school that will allow smooth transition back to a school in the home country if you are planning on heading back before the children have completed their education.
- You can choose to educate your children in a local school or an international school. International schools allow for easier transition back into your home country, but costs can be prohibitive. Some schools offer full or part scholarships.
- Entrance requirements may differ, especially for local schools, so research this well in advance.

- Bilingual local schools that offer courses in, say, English as well as the local language give your children the ability to phase-in their language skills.
- If there are not any suitable secondary schools available, an alternative could be a boarding school either in your home country or another location.
- For those expats not on a full ‘expat’ package, the cost of education should be one of the first things planned for.
- Prepare a forecast of the cost of your children’s education for the next five years.

4

EXPATLAND BANKING

Banking is an area that presents a range of alternatives for expats to think about. These include establishing a local bank account; having an offshore bank account in an offshore financial centre; or keeping your home country bank account.

Local Bank Account

Generally speaking, it is more expensive to access your home country bank account for cash via the ATM network – hence a local account is an advantage. Also most employers will require a local bank account to pay in wages. Indeed, some institutions will not accept foreign bank payments for their services.

In essence, establishing a local bank account is essential if you are moving to Expatland to work.

Setting up the Account

Often local banks will ask for information from you that might seem surprising, such as questionnaires about your credit history or solvency and other queries. Part of this is normal background checking due to global changes in the areas of anti-money laundering.

Unlike parts of Expatland where opening an account can be straightforward – for example, Singapore – you should be aware that in other countries the process can take hours or even days while information is verified and dealt with by the bank.

If your home country bank account has a presence in Expatland, you may be able to begin work on setting up an account before you arrive. That way you can hit the ground running and access cash shortly after you arrive.

Using the same bank in your home country and in Expatland can make transfers faster and less costly.

It makes sense to look for a local bank that may offer services tailored towards expats, such as translation services or specialists who understand your home country culture.

Using a local bank account will make things such as paying for basic in-country utilities much easier. While the rules for establishing a bank account will vary across Expatland, most banks will allow expats who are employed to open an account.

This will not usually include credit cards unless the income to be earned is of sufficient level to justify the provision of a credit card. Debit cards, however, are more readily attainable.

Some parts of Expatland will require you to be registered for tax purposes before opening a bank account, and some banks will also require you to make a small deposit as part of the bank account opening process. In fact, some institutions will not accept foreign bank payments for their services.

What is the Best Account Type for You?

For most expats, it is worth having an everyday or current account as well as a savings account.

Some expats have been surprised to find that account types that paid interest in their home country do not pay interest in Expatland. Hence having an everyday account that receives salary on a regular basis, together with a savings account that pays interest on funds that accumulate is advisable.

Generally speaking, savings accounts are easy to open, but they do not offer the types of features of other accounts, such as overdraft facilities.

Your Home Country Bank Account

It can also be a benefit to maintain your existing home country bank account if you receive regular investment income. This may be because of lower costs on bank fees and/or avoiding timing delays with sending money overseas.

If you have a home country mortgage, then keeping income in the home currency and in the same location is more efficient.

Before you leave your home country, it can be a legal requirement to tell your bank that you are leaving as some countries have a withholding tax regime that requires them to withhold tax on bank interest payable to non-residents.

Also remember to ask your existing bank about charges for using a foreign ATM and what costs are for exchanging currency or accessing other bank services.

In the event that you move to Expatland and wish to close your home country bank account, you should ensure that alternative arrangements are made in relation to regular periodical payments, such as insurance policies or mortgage payments.

There is a wide degree of variability with respect to global banking practices. Hence you should not expect your relationship with your bank in your home country to be the same as you will experience in Expatland. Not only are the products and services likely to be different but the way you interact with your bank could also be different.

While it is usual to use personal cheques in the US and other countries, in some locations, such as Singapore, there are other forms for payment such as 'giro'. The giro is made out to an account number rather than a name, and submitted to the bank for payment rather than being sent to the payee.

Offshore Banking

Generally speaking, offshore banking refers to banking undertaken in offshore financial centres (OFC) such as Jersey, Hong Kong, the Cayman Islands, Bermuda or Cyprus. Also some countries like Singapore have significant offshore financial facilities, although they are not tax havens as such.

Leading economies such as the UK also have sophisticated offshore banking offerings, but more often than not OFCs are found in very low tax countries.

In general, a tax haven is common parlance for those locations that have no tax on income or capital gains. These locations can be chosen by expats and business people alike as a place to establish a company or trust to manage their assets.

An example of a thriving economy, which is regarded as a tax haven, is the United Arab Emirates. There are no taxes imposed on income or capital.

Provided no income tax or capital gains taxes are being unlawfully avoided, the use of 'tax havens' can present a number of benefits. Some of these include:

- Protection of wealth due to aspects of their domestic legislation. Protecting wealth is important for those expats involved in business or family disputes;

- Relative anonymity, which is useful in commercial situations where assets need to be held on a nominee basis;

- Ease of regulation in terms of funds management; and

- Access to specialist skills due to a concentration of qualified professionals.

Most residents of Expatland can easily access the market for an OFC via the internet or by contacting their banker. They do not have to visit the OFC often.

While offshore banking is perceived as being the domain of wealthy expats, many expats can open an account in places like Hong Kong and Singapore or the Cayman Islands relatively easily and without much fanfare.

It's important to note, however, that using such tax havens to hold assets has some disadvantages. These are:

- Some banks in tax havens can be less secure. Recent examples include Iceland, where the economic crisis saw investors lose funds because of the banks leveraging far too much debt. And while some investors were able to have their funds returned many others remained out of pocket.

- If you are a foreign investor in another country, you may have less protection than if you were a resident of the country.

- Understand what the extent of any guarantee would be in the event of a default. Some compensation schemes fall short of what would be expected. There are accounts of a particular bank in Asia that, following the collapse of Lehman Brothers, refused to compensate depositors even though the customers believed the funds were guaranteed under the banking regime of the country.

- Possibility of data loss. In a recent high profile case involving a banker in Luxembourg, customer data was released to European tax authorities for a 'reward'. While the vast majority of these customers were fully complying with their home country tax obligations, private information was shared with parties who had no right to the information. Therefore, small country OFCs do have some issues that have to be considered carefully when it comes to their banking regimes.

- Taxation Information Exchange Agreements (TIEAs). Many offshore jurisdictions now have procedures to allow various governments to have access to information if they suspect a person may be attempting to avoid paying tax. There are moves to take action against those jurisdictions that refuse to co-operate.

A TIEA is a bilateral agreement that has been negotiated and signed between two nations to formalise an official system for the exchange of information relating to taxes. There are more than 2000 TIEAs in force globally. These allow for the free exchange of financial tax information irrespective of differences in either country's requirements or definitions of a predicate crime of money laundering.

However, it must be recognised that generally information will only be provided if a proper request is made that follows all the treaty provisions, which require that the requesting party first make a prima facie case. In some cases, an application must be made to the high court of the country to determine if the request has been properly complied with.

Various countries tailor the conditions that would give effect to the requirement to exchange information and limit the categories of data that would have to be transferred. Generally speaking, fishing expeditions that seek to obtain information about persons undertaking a certain type of activity are not permitted.

The governments of many countries are seeking to enter into taxation information exchange agreements, which will provide that a country seeking information on the assets of its citizens in another country can make a request of a foreign government.

The foreign government can then approach banks, financial institutions and trust companies to determine if a named person has assets located in the jurisdiction. This exchange of information is a powerful deterrent to the practice of tax evasion.

JITSIC

JITSIC (Joint International Tax Shelter Information Centre) is a relatively unknown body. It was established to co-ordinate efforts of member countries and to help discover cases of international tax avoidance. The efforts of JITSIC are directed to combating tax evasion in real time.

Current members of JITSIC include Australia, Canada, Japan, the UK, the US, South Korea and China, while France and Germany are participating as observers.

JITSIC delegates plans and discusses the latest tax patterns and trends that occur across their jurisdictions. Publicly, delegates of JITSIC note their achievements as deterrence and exchanging information. By having the program, JITSIC sends a clear signal to global tax professionals about member country's intentions to identify and curtail abusive tax arrangements on an international scale. By exchanging information regularly, member nations pursue a number of schemes such as foreign tax credit generators, structured financing, hybrid instruments and private equity cases.

Main Offshore Financial Centres

There are several offshore financial centres that are very popular, and these are in Asia, Europe and the Caribbean.

Each OFC generally develops expertise in a particular area. For example, in Bermuda it is usually related to insurance, and in the case of the Cayman Islands, it is funds management. In Cyprus, the OFCs have special skills in the area of tourism, trust and business administration, as well as oil and gas. In the Cook Islands, the OFC expertise usually lies with asset and wealth protection. The Cayman Islands and the Cook Islands are very popular with investors from the US.

Many offshore banks offer higher rates of interest to attract deposits. They will also generally make interest payments to customers with no withholding of taxes. In addition, they will provide a private banker to service the account and explain wealth management strategies and products to assist expats.

They are usually very well-regulated and as such their internal governance procedures ensure that only well-educated and highly trained private bankers work for the offshore bank.

Keep in mind that government regulation in high tax countries can impose greater costs on banks that result in less return to the customer.

Banking Tips

These banking tips are a guideline and will give you some helpful pointers on your way to Expatland.

1. Establish a bank account in Expatland as soon as possible.

2. Ask local co-workers and also expats for a recommendation.

3. Don't assume the foreign bank operates similarly to your home country bank – staff may not speak your language or understand your thinking – and processes may be different. It is best to proceed slowly and understand products and services thoroughly before proceeding.

4. Understand the role of the bank manager, which may still be of some importance in various parts of Expatland.

5. Build a relationship with the bank and establish a credit rating by making regular deposits into your local account. This may involve setting up a regular payment from your home country to your new account at Expatland.

6. Understand the bank's technology platform and your options to interact with it.

7. Expatland banking is often built on relationships that have to be developed and maintained.

8. Try to avoid going overdrawn, as this may be illegal in some parts of Expatland.

AT A GLANCE

- Establishing a local bank account is essential in Expatland.
- Local banks may ask for information that might seem surprising, such as your credit history or solvency. Part of this is normal background checks because of global changes in the areas of anti-money laundering.
- Opening a bank account in Expatland can take hours or days while the bank verifies your information.
- Look for a local bank that offers services tailored towards expats, such as translation services.
- Using the same bank in your home country and in Expatland can make transfers faster and less costly. It will also help you access cash in Expatland without delays.
- In some parts of Expatland you will be required to be registered for tax purposes before opening a bank account.
- Some banks will require you to make a small deposit as part of the bank account opening process.
- Try to avoid going overdrawn, as this may be illegal in some parts of Expatland.
- For most expats, having an everyday or current account as well as a savings account is best.
- Before exiting your home country, you may be legally required to tell your bank that you are leaving as some countries have a withholding tax regime that requires them to withhold tax on bank interest payable to non-residents.

- Ask your existing bank about charges for using a foreign ATM and what costs are for exchanging currency or accessing other bank services.
- Provided no income tax or capital gains taxes are being unlawfully avoided, the use of 'tax havens' can present a number of benefits.
- Many offshore banks (Offshore Financial Centres) offer higher rates of interest to attract deposits.

5

EXPATLAND FINANCES

The cost of living is of major importance to you and your family in looking at whether you will be better off in Expatland. The cost of living in different parts of Expatland varies widely and is affected by many factors beyond your control.

Just one of these for example is, say, the effect of tax rises in Expatland. Those countries in Expatland that may have higher national debt as a percentage of GDP might seek to raise taxes shortly after your arrival.

This tax rise – whether indirect or direct – may affect your cost of living in a very short period of time. It is therefore important for you to prepare a budget.

Preparing a Budget

One of the key action items when venturing into Expatland is to prepare a budget. (In Appendix F, 'Budget Template', we set out our budget template for your use in this area.)

If you arrive in Expatland without full-time work, you should ensure that you have made provision for the cost of living until you secure full-time employment. Remember the old adage that 'the more free time you have, the more time you have to spend money'.

Costs in many parts of Expatland may be cheaper than your home country for some items such as staple foods, but other costs may be much higher, such as alcohol or other discretionary goods.

Delays in finding full-time employment can quickly erode capital buffers designed to cover the cost of living. We have seen situations where clients lose employment in Expatland, and rather than returning home, stay in Expatland looking for alternate employment.

This strategy has some merit, as it may be easier to find employment by remaining in the market looking for work rather than looking for work from your home country. Nonetheless, the cost of remaining in an expensive city such as Hong Kong (where education expenses for children are relatively high) has to be evaluated against the cost of returning to your home country.

Thus having a provision for the cost of living during your entire period in Expatland makes sense. For this reason, in our template in Appendix F we have a separate line item 'provision for living costs'.

If you have no separate provision established, then working towards having a six-month cost of living buffer to remain in Expatland with no employment income is wise.

When you are preparing your budget, consider these points:

- What are the additional expenses that you will be expected to incur while in Expatland? For example, school fees for your children or more significant medical costs.

- Will your spouse transition from working to not working? If your spouse or partner has more time on their hands they are likely to spend more money.

- If the tax rate is lower in Expatland than in your home country, then it is likely there will be much more cash floating around and this may lead to a temptation to spend more on expenditures like travel and entertainment.

- Understand the weekly cost of your consumables as lower costs in some areas may be outweighed by higher costs in others. For example, in some parts of Expatland you will need air conditioning running all year round and this has to be budgeted for.

- When moving to Expatland clearly understand what relocation costs will be covered by your employer and what costs are not. Depending upon your employer you may be able to negotiate cost of flights to Expatland, importation of furniture and belongings plus allowances for in-country costs such as a maid.

Only when you have fully understood the complete cost of living can you understand the financial benefit potential of moving to Expatland.

Let us now examine some of the main cost items ahead of you in Expatland:

- **Accommodation**: Will your employer cover the cost of accommodation? Is there a specific allowance in your salary package for this item? If so, then how realistic is the allowance you receive in Expatland?

  Some parts of Expatland commonly require you to pay rent in advance – sometimes up to six months – when you first arrive. So although your employer may cover you on a 'monthly' basis, you may have to fund the initial payment or security deposit and this may require some out of pocket funding in advance. It is important to be clear about that.

Similarly, if you are not renting furnished accommodation, you may need to buy furniture and appliances. Depending upon the location in Expatland, this can be expensive. An alternative is to import your own furniture from home.

Other costs associated with accommodation include utility bills and property taxes. While sometimes these costs can be lower in emerging countries than in your home country, it is worth understanding issues around consistency and access to infrastructure services, internet, cable TV, gas and other costs. In some parts of Expatland, service providers of the utilities are privately owned and costs can fluctuate widely.

- **Car**: Depending upon the location of your employment, you may not require a car in Expatland. As such, budgeting for this expense may not be needed. However, if public transport is inconvenient or you want to have the freedom to travel as you wish, then the cost of buying or leasing a car has to be considered.

  Some parts of Expatland, such as Singapore, impose significant costs for using private vehicles. Importing your car may be an option worth considering.

  It is also important for you to factor in other costs, such as insurance, fuel and maintenance along with the initial challenge of obtaining a driving licence as most parts of Expatland will not allow you to continue driving on your home country licence.

- **Education**: For expats travelling with children, this is usually one of the more significant expense categories. These expenses refer to all school fees from kindergarten to university.

  In some locations in Expatland you will be required to fund a bond for your children to secure them a place in a private school. Other parts of Expatland will allow your children to use local schools at little or no cost. Make a note to research how effective the local free education is, because if attendance at a local school is not comparable to your home country education system it may be hard for children to fit into the education system in their home country. For this reason, in key markets many expats prefer private school education.

  University costs can be significant and readers with teenage children close to finishing school might consider if it is appropriate for children to return to home country universities.

  Regardless of your location in Expatland, funding secondary and higher education expenses is something that should be budgeted for so that you are not confronted with expenses all at the same time.

- **Food**: The cost of buying brands you are familiar with in Expatland is generally higher than local brands as these have been imported in many cases. Hence it may be worth testing local produce to keep control of this item on the budget.

- **Medical and health costs**: As discussed earlier, having the right medical insurance in place in Expatland is essential. It is very important that you are aware of the standard of the local healthcare system and if you qualify as a non-citizen to use it. Keep in mind that costs vary widely throughout Expatland for both pharmaceutical and medical services.

- **Leisure and entertainment**: This item covers leisure expenses, generally for the amusement and relaxation of you and your family. It may cover enjoyable activities such as movie tickets, trips to amusement parks or exhibitions and the like. Generally if you have a maid in Expatland, you will have more free time and this can often lead to higher entertainment and amusement expenses.

- **Restaurants**: This is an area that most expats spend more on in Expatland. The existence of more after-tax salary tends to lead to higher spending in both family restaurants and fast food outlets.

  Our suggestion is to do your research and look for those restaurants that offer you a reasonably priced night out, particularly as you are likely to be eating out much more often.

- **Liquor and tobacco**: In certain parts of Expatland, such as in the Middle East, where alcohol is prohibited in public areas, spending on these items is almost zero. Having said that, some parts of Expatland allow alcohol consumption in expats' residential compounds. In the Middle East, some of the larger expat compounds have a bar and they usually serve home-brewed alcohol. Some of our client Expats have regaled us with stories about how they learned to make alcohol. Thus your cost in these areas may be very little.

  However, in some parts of Expatland, governments may be attempting to limit the use of alcohol and cigarettes and thus prices may be artificially higher. In other countries, like Singapore, alcohol is much more expensive than in the West.

- **Public transport**: While not usually an exorbitant cost, it is nonetheless important to understand how you and your family will get to and from work and school. The cost of public transport or taxis can soon add up.

- **Credit rating**: In some parts of Expatland, you will not be able to obtain credit facilities without a credit rating. Therefore establishing a credit rating when you move to Expatland is essential if you wish to apply for a credit card or loan. For example, in the US your credit rating will impact your ability to borrow and the rate of interest you will pay.

All parts of Expatland have their own procedures to follow in order to establish a credit rating. Indeed in some parts of Expatland loans to certain types of visa holders may not be available.

It is worth undertaking a review of the rules around credit and loan facilities before your arrive. Retaining your home country credit cards and debt facilities is often advisable until you have assessed the viability of obtaining such facilities in Expatland.

It is generally the case that an expat who is not registered with the government in Expatland and who does not possess some form of tax file number or social security ID will find it impossible to obtain credit in Expatland.

When you are registered with the relevant government authority – in some cases city, state and federal authorities – opening a bank account is the next step in establishing a credit rating.

It may be the case that having a history with a bank in your home country facilitates you to form a relationship with the same bank in Expatland. In other cases, when you initially open a bank account the transactions you can undertake may be restricted, such as in the US.

Remember that credit cards are useful for covering short-term expenses, but they can quickly become a debt trap.

In other parts of Expatland, different banks have slightly differing bank account security measures. For example, some may make you wait a period of time before clearing an overseas cheque. Therefore, if you are receiving a foreign payment by cheque it may be necessary to establish cheque clearing times.

In other parts of Expatland, you may have to make a minimum opening deposit to establish your bona fides.

Other banks require you to establish a term deposit account and then will give you a credit card. The deposit account is held as security until you have established that you are good customer. After a period of time this deposit is then released. Keep in mind that using your credit card to pay for small items often helps you to establish a good credit rating.

Some business clients find that establishing merchant facilities usually requires placement of a security deposit. For those expats who are accustomed to reasonably flexible home market banking systems, this can come as shock.

It can feel as if it is a privilege to have a bank account in some parts of Expatland!

As noted earlier, if you keep your credit card from your home country and although you may have changed your mailing address, you should be aware that on occasion your transaction may be declined as you are overseas.

If you are offered credit cards in Expatland, consider accepting them as a back-up source of funding rather than an essential part of day-to-day living.

In Expatland you might consider using a local card with a small credit balance to buy goods online. Generally speaking, expats arrive in Expatland with credit cards from their arrival countries that have higher credit limits. This may mean that use of a card with a higher credit limit offers the opportunity for others to access more of your funds fraudulently.

Moving Currency

Movements in exchange rates can make significant impact on your time as an expat. There are a number of issues to consider here. Key among these is knowing where you want to retire to and what your home currency asset base is.

Hence if you are an Australian expat and you plan to retire in Australia, then while in Expatland it may make sense to regularly and systematically transfer funds back to Australia. This will mitigate currency impacts that may prevail at the time of your return.

Building up large holdings of, say, Japanese yen or English pounds may cause issues in moving those savings back to Australia at the end of your time in Expatland.

It's worthwhile considering if you plan on receiving foreign income streams to sustain you while you are in Expatland. If this is the case, then variations in daily exchange rates can have a positive or negative impact on your income in Expatland. This is something that needs to be thought about before moving to Expatland.

In some cases, those who have moved without their families might consider requesting that part of their salary is paid in their home currency and part is paid in the currency of Expatland. This is an attempt to spread the currency obligation between the jurisdictions of expenditure.

For example, it may not be ideal to be transferring a weakening currency back to a home jurisdiction to pay your mortgage and other expenses that remain payable in the home country. Understanding where the monthly expenses are likely to be incurred is important in this respect.

In other cases, if you negotiate that your salary is paid in the currency of Expatland then that should generally cover the cost of living appropriately.

This issue of building up savings in a foreign currency and then transferring that value back to the home market in which you plan to retire is an important one.

Hence using debt in Expatland to acquire assets in your home market may be one way to manage the issue. (This will be discussed in Chapter 6, 'Expatland Financial Planning'.)

Various parts of Expatland have different fundamentals that make their economy work. For example, some parts of Expatland are rich in natural resources, while others are rich in intellectual capital. This affects currency markets.

For example, those expats travelling to commodity-based economies can find that currency broadly parallels the demands for the export commodities of those markets.

Other markets that are heavily reliant on tourism will be more dependent on the flows of that industry to determine currency movements.

My view is that when looking at global wealth management and currency allocation, an emphasis on your retirement country currency should remain a focus point.

Foreign Currency Transfers

Transferring foreign currency from banks can be expensive for many expats, as the value received will vary from day to day.

If transferring money is essential, then it can be advisable to transfer larger amounts to your home account as banks usually charge per transaction. Please be aware of the fact that a currency exchange rate variation may last a number of years.

When you are making a foreign currency transfer always try to obtain the best exchange rate you can. It is not our function to nominate service providers here, but a good way of proceeding is to seek out a reputable currency broker that you can trust via referrals from other expats or recommendations from private bankers in Expatland.

There are numerous ways of moving money abroad. So remember to do your research. Here are some of the common ways of proceeding:

International Bank Transfers

Your home country bank may have an internet platform that allows for small transfers of funds from your home country to Expatland. In that case, you might want to move home country rental income or investment income to Expatland to meet regular expenses.

If this is so, then depending upon the fees involved, accumulating income on a quarterly or six-monthly basis may be more cost effective than transferring weekly or monthly.

For those banks that don't allow the transfer online, then usually you can set up authorisations to voice call or fax instructions.

As a guide, international bank transfers take one to two working days.

Another option is establishing a regular telegraphic transfer payment facility with your bank for a set amount.

At the outset it is important to get the transaction established properly. Some banks required a swift code or an ABA (American Bankers Association number) or IBAN (International Bank Account Number). Whatever the requirement, your bank will be able to assist you

The benefit of this approach is that you will not have to manually do these transfers and you can have some peace of mind that a system has been established to move home country income to Expatland.

In terms of charges, it would be normal to pay a flat fee per transaction with some form of percentage fee for the currency conversion. Remember that transferring larger sums less frequently is cheaper than transferring lesser amounts more often.

ATM Withdrawals

Given the improvements in technology, many expats are tempted to use their home country Visa or MasterCards to access cash from their bank accounts back home.

While this is quick and easy, it is worth understanding the fees applicable because sometimes there can be significant fees for this type of transaction. There may also be limits in place in terms of how much cash can be withdrawn via the ATM network.

Also please be aware that cash withdrawals from your credit card pay not only the higher interest rate from the credit card provider, but also the fee for using the ATM network – as well as a fee for the currency conversion.

Try to obtain details from your local bank of what charges will be involved when you convert your home country currency into Expatland currency through the ATM network.

Foreign Currency Brokers

Foreign currency brokers can offer significant advantages over banks. These include the following:

- They can offer you a better rate than your bank. This is because they have access to the interbank rate and in general lower cost structures. Generally speaking, these savings can vary from between 1–4 per cent on the exchange rate alone, and these specialists do not usually charge fees for transmitting the funds overseas.

- Generally the process is clearer.

- While most banks require you to accept a transfer on the date they process your transaction, a broker can price a transfer by allowing you to set the rate you want ahead of time.

- You are generally able to set a rate using a forward exchange rate contract. A foreign exchange contract is an agreement between you and the currency broker to exchange one currency for another at an agreed exchange rate on an agreed settlement date.

On the settlement date there is a physical delivery of one currency in exchange for the other currency, and the amount you pay in the currency you deliver is determined by the agreed exchange rate.

What are Exchange Rates?

An exchange rate is the price at which one currency can be bought or sold and which is expressed in terms of another currency.

All quotations are made up of two currencies: The base currency and the terms currency. These form what is known as the 'currency pair'. The first currency in the quoted currency pair is known as the base currency and the second is referred to as the terms currency.

A quotation shows how many units of the terms currency will equal one unit of the base currency.

The following are the usual features available from a currency broker:

- You can fix the rate of exchange on foreign currency transactions on a specified date or for a period of time.
- They are available for any business dealing in one or more foreign currencies; you get a fixed rate of exchange for the sale or purchase of a set amount of foreign currency.
- Your rate of exchange is guaranteed, enabling you to determine what your costs or income will be.
- The value of transactions in the future can be accurately calculated.
- Contracts are available in most major currencies.
- You pay the foreign exchange rate that is based on the spot rate on the day of the deal.
- A forward exchange contract is binding and will have to be cancelled if you don't use it; this may result in a profit or loss depending on the exchange rate on the day of cancellation.
- If you use a market watch service you can then let your currency broker know your planned rate. The broker can then call you when the rate is reached.

Impacts on Exchange Rates

Movements in the exchange rate can make a significant difference to the value of your funds when moving money overseas. It is therefore vital to time your currency exchange appropriately in order to obtain the most for your base currency.

Common factors impacting exchange rates are:

- Economic data releases
- Announcements on inflation
- Announcements on unemployment.

A government announcement on interest rates, for example, could have a major impact on exchange rates. Notification that interest rates will rise generally increases the value of a base currency.

Most currency brokers provide additional services to their clients. They can assist you to follow the news in the market and their updates can provide an insight into how the market is moving.

In some cases it can be worthwhile holding off making a transfer in the days before or after an announcement if there is uncertainty in the market and the size of your transfer is material to you.

A word of caution: currency brokers are generally smaller than banks, so be sure to conduct some due diligence and obtain comfort from referrals or industry recommendations if you can.

AT A GLANCE

- Planning a budget is highly recommended.
- Have a contingency plan and a financial buffer in the event you become unemployed.
- Credit cards are useful for covering short-term expenses, but they can quickly become a debt trap.
- Consider credit cards in Expatland as a back-up source of funding rather than an essential part of day-to-day living.
- In Expatland consider using a local card with a small credit balance to buy goods online.
- Higher credit limit offers the opportunity for others to access more of your funds fraudulently.
- If you plan to retire in Australia, while in Expatland it may be a good idea to regularly transfer funds back to Australia. This mitigates currency impacts that may prevail at the time of your return.
- Expats whose families remain in the home country could request that part of their salary is paid in their home currency and part is paid in the currency of Expatland. This spreads the currency obligation between the jurisdictions of expenditure.
- When looking at global wealth management and currency allocation, an emphasis on your retirement country's currency should remain a focus point.
- If transferring money is essential, then best to transfer larger amounts to your home account as banks usually charge per transaction.

- Keep in mind that international bank transfers take one to two working days.
- If you use your home country Visa or MasterCard to access cash from their bank accounts back home, sometimes there can be significant fees. There may also be limits to how much cash can be withdrawn via the ATM network.
- Foreign currency brokers can offer significant advantages over banks.
- Movements in the exchange rate can make a significant difference to the value of your funds when moving money overseas. Time your currency exchange appropriately in order to obtain the most for your base currency.

6

EXPATLAND FINANCIAL PLANNING

One of the great challenges upon arrival in Expatland is often how to manage your money. There is no easy answer and it depends upon the complexity of your affairs.

Similar to your home country jurisdiction, financial planning requires a number of steps. The following will serve as a good guideline:

1. **The Client/Planner**: The financial planner defines their responsibilities and yours. They outline who will remunerate them for their services and how. As an expatriate client, you discuss and agree with the planner how long they will work for you and how the decisions concerning your finances will be made. Given that you are generally going to seek broad financial advice, make sure you discuss your global assets and assess how often the relevant planner has worked with clients from your home country.

2. **Goals & Expectations**: Your financial planner will ask all the relevant questions about your finances, your goals (both fiscal and personal) and whether you prefer a high-risk or low-risk strategy, gathering all the appropriate documentation. An additional overlay here is to acknowledge that time horizons for investment as an expatriate client can shift year to year if not more frequently. Generally speaking flexibility is the key.

3. **Analysis & Evaluation**: After gathering all the appropriate information, the financial planner will assess your information and determine the best course of action. This could include examining your assets, liabilities and cash flow, current insurance coverage, investments or tax strategies. As the relationship in Expatland is likely to be a relatively new one, it is prudent to involve advisors from your home country where applicable at the evaluation stage. This ensures that a well-rounded evaluation takes place.

4. **The Financial Plan**: The financial planner offers financial planning recommendations and/or alternatives that address the client's goals based on the information the client provided. The planner reviews the recommendations with the client to allow the client to make informed decisions. The planner listens to client concerns and revises recommendations as appropriate. Again it makes sense to involve your home country accountant and/or lawyer to review the plan where they are qualified to and also act as sounding boards. Given the newness of the relationship, getting independent third-party assessments makes sense.

5. **Implementing the Recommendations**: The financial planner and client agree on how recommendations will be carried out. The planner may carry out the recommendations for the client or serve as a 'coach', co-ordinating the process with the client and other professionals, such as attorneys or stockbrokers. It is usually the case that implementation is done in a phased manner and where funds are invested in too short a period you can miss the benefits of averaging into the market. Other parts of the financial plan, such as personal insurance, is something that is done more promptly

as usually health risk needs to be covered sooner than funds need to be invested.

6. **Monitoring the Plan:** The client and financial planner agree upon who will monitor the client's progress toward goals. If the planner is involved, they should report to the client periodically to review the situation and adjust recommendations as needed.

Source: Investopedia.com

In Expatland, these are the general steps that need to be undertaken.

How to Choose a Financial Planner

However, it is very often the case that financial planners make contact with you and seek you out because they have access to information about recent arrivals into Expatland.

Independent financial advisors often actively seek new clients and offer a wide range of ready-made savings and wealth management products – and insurance products – designed to offer an enticing picture to you.

Just as in your home market, it is clearly the case that financial planning is important and needs to be done in a way that is relevant to your risk profile, your objectives and your medium- and long-term goals.

The challenge in Expatland is that you are new to the country and therefore keen to make new connections, but it is quite easy to make the wrong type of connections.

Most importantly, if a wealth advisor or a financial planner approaches you, you need to consider what their experience and qualifications are. You should obtain two or three written references from clients of theirs and determine how long they have been in the market.

Many regulatory regimes do not require the financial planner to declare their position on what fees they are earning. It has been my experience that financial planners in some Asian markets are under no obligations to declare certain types of fees and very often mislead clients with over-optimistic projections and the full impact of their remuneration from the sale of the product is not known.

Of equal importance is that the perspective of the financial planner has to be the same as your perspective. For example, if you expect to be in Expatland for say 3–5 years, there is little point in going into a 10- or 15-year savings plan.

Often these types of savings plan have annual and lock-in periods that may require a defined or set monthly commitment. The profile of the asset being invested in may not actually be in accord with your risk profile or that of your partner.

In one case, I came across a client who had unwittingly signed up for a 25-year savings plan in one of the Channel Islands. My client was unaware that the commission to be paid to the financial planner would effectively reduce the earnings for the first six years of the product. In that particular case, the client would forfeit contributions if they stopped making monthly contributions for the first 10 years of the product. Worse still, if the client returned to their home country, in this case Australia, the tax consequences of that foreign financial product were horrible. The client would have an Australian tax obligation, but they were unable to access capital from the product to meet their Australian tax bill.

Some clients feel a need to save the tax differential and make the most of the expat experience. This is a most natural and worthy objective for moving to Expatland, which often requires a move away from family and friends. As such, there is a natural temptation to do something to improve your financial position quickly.

However, you should exercise caution and take time to make a considered decision. Consider just three of the following articles on the subject of expats affected by poor financial planning decisions:

ARTICLE 1

Serious Fraud Office and FSA Now Investigating Harlequin (March 2013)

Britain's Serious Fraud Office (SFO) is now investigating Essex-based Harlequin Group regarding its marketing of high-end Caribbean villas linked with a self-investing personal pension product.

Harlequin's business was not regulated by the Financial Services Authority [FSA], which is now writing to all UK financial advisors requesting the details of any client who has invested in the scheme.

At the same time, the Serious Fraud Office and Essex Police are also requesting full details of the transactions involved from anyone who has invested in the Caribbean resort off-plan sales schemes.

The SFO would also like to hear from others inadvertently caught up in the scam, and states that they may request a full witness statement where necessary.

It's known that a subsidiary of Harlequin, Harlequin Properties Thailand, has caused problems and losses to expats in the resort town of Pattaya, using similar methods.

It's believed that thousands of investors have poured their savings into off-plan purchases of condos and villas in the Caribbean and Thailand, many of whom are now in touch with the FSA.

A legal challenge by a group of investors is expected, based on mis-selling of a financial product.

Harlequin CEO David Ames has denied misleading investors and promised that the developments in question will be finished, blaming contractors for the problems.

However, investigation has revealed that, out of 3000 promised homes, only 300 have as yet been completed and interest payments due to investors have now ceased.

Source: http://www.expatsblog.com/news/0703135520/harlequin-under-investigation-by-sfo-and-fsa#sthash.vXZqDVXE.dpuf

ARTICLE 2

Spanish Court to investigate fraud charges issued by Scottish expat against Danish bank, Danske Bank (16 July 2012).

A breakthrough has been reached for defrauded expat Euan Armstrong, 73, whose legal battle against the biggest bank in Denmark has garnered increasing support from similarly affected expats in Spain.

The Fuengirola Court of First Instance has now agreed to investigate his case against Danske Bank after initially dismissing it last year.

As the Olive Press reported, the Scottish expat was left almost penniless when the bank persuaded him to use his €2 million Malaga home as collateral in an equity release scheme.

Meanwhile the Equity Release Victims Association (www.erva.es), set up by Armstrong and Ian Sherdley to warn Brits about such schemes, is now a recommended site by the British Embassy in Madrid.

Source: http://www.theolivepress.es/spain-news/2012/07/16/fuengirola-court-to-investigate-fraud-charges-issued-by-scottish-expat-against-the-largest-danish-bank/

ARTICLE 3

British Expats in Indonesia in Financial Con (9 August 2012)

A British expat conned his fellow expatriates in Indonesia out of $800,000 according to the Serious Fraud Office (SFO). The man in question was Alan Edwin Gardner, and he was responsible for executing a brilliant financial con – however, his fraud eventually caught up with him and we're pleased to tell you that he was imprisoned for his fraudulent activities.

According to the SFO website: 'In total, five investors from [the expat] community, all involved in the petro-chemical industry in the region, were drawn into the scheme. One investor was shown a fabricated table of figures showing a growth of a $100,000 investment to $151,000 over a three-month period. To allay scepticism of the returns set out in the table, assurances were given that access to this fund had previously been the exclusive privilege of banks, corporations, large brokerages and other financial institutions and that it was now open to private investors who could be confident "in the validity of the opportunity given that

International Banks alone trade in excess of $US 15 trillion dollars daily on the money markets".'

Once investors were introduced to the scheme, Gardner would deal with the applications, create the documents and instruct them to send funds to bank accounts in Switzerland and the UK that he controlled. The funds were extracted almost immediately; the pattern of withdrawals strongly suggesting that there was no real intention to invest on behalf of his clients. One investor lost as much as $357,000. In total, Gardner's scheme pulled in almost $820,000.

Believe it or not, it was other legitimate and genuine financial advisers who blew this scheme out of the water. They heard about it on the expat grapevine and were able to protect many other expats from being conned by alerting the SFO about Gardner's activities.

In 2009 Gardner was sentenced to six years in prison for his dodgy dealings.

However … how were intelligent and affluent expats conned by this man? He offered them 48% returns on their investment a year – come on!! Doesn't that sound too good to be true to you? Yes? Well that's clearly because it was … and there endeth the lesson!"

Source: http://www.expatmoneywatch.com/british-expats-in-indonesia-in-fin ancial-con/

Questions to Ask a Financial Planner

As you can understand from these horror stories, the decision to choose a financial planner is not one to be taken lightly. It is very important and great care should be taken before the person is selected. Personally, I would ask the financial planner to highlight certain strategies that they have used in other cases, and I would always make sure that I obtain relevant feedback.

It is also very useful to know where the financial planner has been educated and what their academic results were. Enquire what their qualifications are as well. A financial planner in all cases should be prepared to be quite open and transparent with you about the best-case scenario.

As an example, let us assume you have moved to Expatland and you have a monthly savings capacity of US$5000 per month. If you plan to be in Expatland for five years, based on your forecast cash flows, let us assume that means you can save approximately US$300,000. A range of options could be discussed about what products could be suited to a five-year time horizon given your level of savings.

A financial planner should present you with a sensitivity analysis so that best- and worst-case scenarios can be presented and the flexibility of any plan should be considered, such as what happens if you need to leave Expatland suddenly; what if there is a period of unemployment; and what if sudden expenses present themselves.

These and other relevant questions need to be identified and considered before a fixed regular commitment is made to a financial plan. It is also the case that many expats have assets in their home country or other countries, and the financial planner needs to understand and appreciate these.

Let's take this example: A client who has three or four investment properties with US dollar exposure may already have enough of that particular exposure.

Hence if the financial plan does not consider this and indeed offer investments in the same sector and the same currency, you should ask some questions and consider whether you are really being given options that are appropriate for you.

It is important to communicate your existing assets and liability position to the financial planner, and you need to fully understand what recommendation should be made to you. Consideration around tax and the tax impact of taking investments in Expatland back to your home country is also of vital importance.

If a financial planner works as part of a broader dealer group or network and you become dissatisfied with the services of the planner, you need to know if there is some form of complaint arbitration. The decision to make a new connection with a professional such as a financial planner is important, and you should consider references from complementary professions like chartered accountants, lawyers or bankers. If the person comes recommended by a professional in one of these industries, that is a good sign.

If you are using a chartered accountant or a lawyer in Expatland, you will need to clarify if there is a pre-existing relationship between these two parties. Moving to Expatland is most often a financial decision, and as such the importance of getting the financial planning aspect absolutely right cannot be overstated.

Building Your Wealth Overseas

As I have just mentioned, one of the prime motivations for moving to Expatland is to build wealth. As such, how you manage your finances is one of the most critical decisions you need to make.

While financial planning in Expatland is similar to your home country, there are a few obvious differences. These include the following:

- Your length of stay in Expatland is often unknown or subject to change.
- Your investment advisory networks in Expatland are generally not the same as in your home country.
- The culture of investment advisors or financial planners and their attitude to client service and the financial planning process may be different from your home country.
- The legal regime that protects you from poor or ill-considered advice may be fundamentally different from your home country.

While in Australia the Six Step Financial Planning Process is relatively well known and regarded, this type of rigour may not be applied in Expatland. (See Appendix E, 'The Six Step Financial Planning List'.)

As a result here are some additional points for you to think about when considering financial planning in Expatland:

1. When leaving a jurisdiction, consider your tax position carefully as it is likely that there will be departure taxation issues. For example, you may be due a tax refund if tax has been withheld at a higher rate than you may be required to pay based on the full year.

2. Alternatively, some countries, such as Australia, impose a capital gains tax on assets you held at the departure date.

3. It is advisable to retain your home country bank account. Retaining this account will allow you to pay bills that continue in your home country.

4. Do not cancel your home country insurance policies until you have had your cover in Expatland completely implemented. It may be the case that premiums are more expensive in Expatland, so please examine the options before cancelling the policy.

5. Establish a bank account in a third country if that does not cause adverse tax consequences for you in Expatland. It is sometimes an advantage to have the flexibility of being able to receive income in a third location – not in the home country or arrival country.

6. It is important to check whether banks in Expatland offer appropriate levels of capital protection compared to your home country banking system.

7. Do your research before making any investment and, generally speaking, you might consider it prudent not to invest all your funds with one financial institution.

8. If you select a quality private banking institution, this may offer you more advantages than lesser-known private banks.

9. If you have a focus on share trading, consider which companies offer suitable technology platforms.

10. Even if Expatland does not impose personal taxes on your income, it may be worth maintaining contributions into your home country national pension plan.

11. When you arrive in Expatland, establish a local bank account with a reserve sufficient to provide funding in case of emergencies, such as loss of employment or poor health.

12. We do not advise you to join an overseas pension scheme before you have conducted appropriate due diligence on the fund and its management team.

13. Make sure you understand all the costs associated with overseas pension schemes.

14. In the event you do not completely understand the arrival country private pension plan scheme, then do not invest before you are satisfied.

15. Be careful about making long-term commitments in Expatland as plans and circumstances change and families grow and their needs shift.

16. An investment decision you made seven years ago would probably not be so appropriate now. The central point here is that most expats may not be in a position to foresee long-term what the best financial decision is, because change is always occurring. Therefore, making a medium- to long-term legal commitment to a particular savings products has to be handled with care and attention.

17. My experience has been that clients have occasionally committed themselves to investment plans costing hundreds

or thousands of dollars a month while other financial loans and obligations remain unpaid.

If the level of tax you are paying in Expatland is much lower than in your home country, it can make financial sense to establish a periodical payment from your Expatland bank account to transfer the funds to a savings account so you can build your financial resources. At the appropriate time, you can then invest the surplus funds as they build up.

Consider diversification of both asset classes and foreign currency holdings carefully.

Without attempting to provide specific comment here, the following categories of assets are worth considering:

- Home country real estate
- Expatland real estate
- Home country currency
- Foreign currency
- Home country listed shares
- International listed shares
- Home country managed funds
- International managed funds
- Home country bonds

- International bonds
- Home country alternative investments
- International alternative investments.

While the temptation may be to continually re-invest in your home country in all asset classes, our advice is to speak to quality private bankers working for reputable global private banks and/or independent financial advisors who can help you understand the following:

1. Your risk profile
2. Your ideal asset allocation
3. Your short-term, medium-term and long-term objectives
4. Portfolios suited to your life circumstances
5. Portfolios that are flexible (important because you now live in Expatland).

What Can Go Wrong?

Generally speaking, our view is if you consider what can go wrong and make plans for an emergency, then if a misfortune occurs a plan has been made. This makes dealing with it much simpler.

Therefore, our view is that if you have a financial plan that covers risks and suits your objectives and, most importantly, is documented and regularly reviewed, then you are well on your way to building wealth.

Independent Financial Advisors

In some parts of Expatland, the independent financial advisor (IFA) can provide good personalised service. While they are usually not part of a major private bank or institution, they can offer tailored financial advice across a wide range of products. Often they are authorised representatives of a larger firm or dealer group.

The dealer group provides them with authority to act on its behalf and to market products and services that have been carefully considered and examined by the dealer group. However, there are some pitfalls to consider when dealing with independent financial advisors. Some of these are:

- As Expatland is a highly mobile and fluid market, your IFA may themselves move around and after a few years you may be left without anyone you know in the dealer group that originally advised you on your financial plan. Hence you should always check what back up for servicing you exists if the IFA leaves their dealer group.

- A colleague or acquaintance may have introduced you to an IFA or the IFA may call you based on an introduction from a contact you know. While that is not a 'cold call' you should still always put the IFA through your own probity and due diligence checks.

- Despite the warm, effusive nature of an IFA's personality, many clients have been let down by particular IFAs who 'sold' products that were not appropriate for them. Often it is not until a few years have elapsed that you can see the downside of poor asset allocation.

- Usually good IFAs do not have to call prospects because they are busy dealing with either referrals from existing clients or existing clients.

- Focus on the strategy of the IFA rather than their personality. Recently we met a new client, who having invested with an IFA in Hong Kong, was lamenting that they had suffered a 50 per cent loss of capital in an IFA's portfolio following the 2008 crash. Only now in 2014 is it close to where it was. They commented that they had not fully understood the principle of volatility or the portfolio of sophisticated products that their IFA had recommended to them.

- The risk of relying on one IFA's recommendations has to be weighed against the protection measures and back up that supports a private banker in a major financial institution. While it may be difficult at first glance to understand the differences between an IFA and a private banker working for a major financial institution, it is our experience that banks offer a better level of protection for clients in the case of misconduct than a dealer group's management of certain rogue IFAs.

- We have heard of a number of cases over the years of IFAs not matching the risk of the portfolio with the client's risk profile.

- In fact, a number of years ago a new client to our firm was the victim of overcharging by an IFA in Asia. After spending quite a lot of time and money with a solicitor representing the client, I saw the regulators in the market 'pass the buck' in this case and refuse to get involved as the ultimate funds were invested in a well-known island just off the UK.

AT A GLANCE

- Manage your money carefully in Expatland. A good financial plan and financial planner is important.
- Many regulatory regimes do not require the financial planner to declare their fees, so find out what their fees and commissions are.
- Often expats cannot foresee long-term residence in Expatland, hence making a medium- to long-term legal commitment to a savings product has to be thought through very carefully.
- Consider the tax impact of taking investments in Expatland back to your home country.
- If your financial planner works as part of a broader dealer group or network, find out if there is some form of complaint arbitration if you become dissatisfied with the individual planner.
- Check what back up for servicing you exists if the independent financial advisor leaves the country or the company.
- When you are leaving a jurisdiction, consider your tax position carefully as it is likely there will be departure taxation issues.
- Consider retaining at least one home country bank account so you can pay continuing bills.
- Continue making home country pension plan payments if possible.

- Check whether banks in Expatland offer appropriate levels of capital protection when compared with your home country banking system.
- Review the rules around credit and loan facilities before you arrive in Expatland.
- Establishing a credit rating when you move to Expatland is essential if you wish to apply for a credit card or loan.
- Financial planners often know who has recently arrived in Expatland. They will seek you out, but make sure you do due diligence.
- Don't keep your assets in your home country or other countries hidden from your financial planner. The financial planner needs to understand those assets to make informed financial recommendations.
- Keep in mind that the legal regime that protects you from poor or ill-considered advice may not be the same as in your home country.
- Keep your home country insurance policies until you have had your cover in Expatland completely implemented and any waiting period has expired. It may be the case that premiums are more expensive in Expatland, so examine the options before cancelling the policy.
- Regarding any overseas pension schemes, conduct appropriate due diligence on the fund and its management team.

7

EXPATLAND ESTATE PLANNING

An unfortunate possibility for an expat and their family would be if there were a death while in Expatland. Such a tragic event can be compounded for the family by not having a properly drafted and considered estate plan.

In general terms, an estate plan is a document that considers what assets/debts go to whom and, if there are young children, who will be their guardians. It considers the executor of the estate, who takes responsibility for the debts and who makes the decisions for the education and maintenance of any young children. It determines what assets, such as heirlooms, should be left to a particular person or family members. If an estate is to continue for a number years, such a document should outline how the estate will actually be managed and maintained in respect to tax and accounting obligations.

CST Tax Advisors and specialist legal counsel have drafted a number of general estate plans and discussed objectives with many expats. In our experience, it's very important that the expat understands the concept of death in Expatland. Would your foreign Will, if there is one, be recognised there? Think about how your Will would be provided and if a local Will is needed and how that can be drafted carefully.

One of the key issues with young children is how they may actually be allowed to leave Expatland in the case of the death of both parents. It may be that a document needs to be filed with a solicitor, showing clear authorisation for grandparents or other relations to be able to make the right decisions in the event of the death of the parents. These documents may need to be stamped and/or filed with the guardian office in Expatland.

It can happen that the executor in one country may find it very difficult to administer the estate and the bulk of the assets if they are held in a different country. It is worthwhile making sure that one executor resides in the country where the deceased lived and worked, or at least a professional executor is appointed as a co-executor to assist in the management and divestment of property under the Will. The bereaved family members may need help from various professionals to manage the sale of assets, the repayment of debts, or the collection of monies owed from government departments. It may be beyond the skill set of the family members to give effect to the Will.

In the case of young children, their proposed guardian may live in another country. This presents issues in terms of which country the children need to move to in order to live with the guardian and how the guardian may need compensation for their time and effort. Ordinarily the guardian would have access to some income of the estate to pay for the income maintenance and other costs incurred for the children's benefit. Where the guardian may have their own children, there should be clarity around whether they can use some money from the estate to increase the size of their house or move house so they can cater for the children of the deceased.

There should also be work undertaken to recognise that the law in the Expatland of the deceased may require those children of a certain age to do national service, which may actually prevent them from leaving.

The objectives of an estate plan are as follows:

1. Assets to be kept are in fact assets that actually exist and should be readily identifiable.

2. Custody of those assets should be passed to a trust that can be created upon death and exist for a defined period of time.

3. If no trust is to be created on death, there should be clarity around who gets which assets and in what proportions.

4. A list of important contacts should be evident in the estate plan, and those contacts should be reviewed and maintained.

5. The executor should be made aware that they are an executor and be readily willing and able to act.

6. Guardians should be made aware that they are to take up this role and be readily willing and able to act.

7. Multiple copies of the Will should exist and be kept in at least two locations with your accountant and your lawyer.

8. The Will should be reviewed on a regular basis.

In the case of larger estates, some private banks offer a service where their trustee professional is able to come in and execute the estate plan.

Expatland Estate Planning

Preparing an estate plan is the most efficient way to give effect to the fair distribution of your assets after your death. Although you may have a Will in your home country, it may have no validity in Expatland and this needs to be understood quickly. Hence obtaining a referral to a specialist estate planner before you arrive in Expatland makes sense as part of your pre-planning.

Failure to have a Will that is legal in Expatland may result in assets being transferred under the laws that prevail in Expatland. If those laws automatically pass on assets to people or relatives that are not in accordance with your wishes, then this prospect should be guarded against.

In Australia in the absence of a proper Will, for example, some states such as New South Wales allow for all relatives to make a claim upon the estate and have your assets divided under a formula approach.

Planning Your Will

Perhaps the most useful starting point for expats with a Will in their home country is to make sure they are aware of the local legislation in Expatland.

Asking yourself the following questions will help you put the right plans in place to protect your loved ones in the event of your demise.

In the case of a single person:

1. Whom do you plan to receive your assets in Expatland and your home country?

2. How do they access your bank accounts and other assets in Expatland?

3. Do you have particular donations or other bequests in mind that you would like covered?

4. Do you have relatives, such as nieces and nephews, whom you would like some of your assets to go to?

5. Are these bequests to people over the age of 18? In some countries they may need to be 21 years old to be recipients.

6. Do you have any siblings whom you wish to receive your estate over other siblings? What are the rules covering this type of favouritism in Expatland? Should you set up a trust beforehand to assist you here?

7. Are you the sole provider for your parents? And what would happen to them in the event of your demise?

8. Who can make the decision to end your life if you are in a comatose state? You may wish to have a living Will in the event that this happens. The document can speak for you by outlining what medical procedures you want to have taken.

9. Do you have an enduring power of attorney that can operate in the event of your demise so that someone can deal with your financial assets to sustain your life, pay bills and so on?

10. Do you have a letter of instruction that can provide a list of instructions for people to follow, such as where your Will may be found?

11. Have you pre-planned your funeral and arranged funding for it?

12. If you have shares in a company or business, is there a business succession plan?

13. Does your accountant or financial advisor have an up-to-date listing of your assets? Are they aware whether you have a safety deposit box or other secure document storage facility?

14. Do you have a list of all organisations in which you are a member, as some of these may provide death benefits as part of their membership?

15. If you have pets, is there a plan for what happens in the event of your demise?

In the case of those with partners:

1. In the event of premature death, how do you safeguard assets for the children if your partner marries again?

2. Who will look after your children if they are minors?

3. What is the long-term plan for funding the children's education?

4. What is the financial position for those taking guardianship custody of children?

5. If your children are left alone in Expatland, what is the process for a relative, your executor or a friend being able to make decisions for them and care for them?

6. Do you understand how minor children can be looked after in Expatland until they are relocated to your home country?

7. Will Expatland allow your older children to leave or will they need to remain and undergo national service? Indeed, in some parts of Expatland children may be required to return for national service. Failure to do so may be a crime.

8. Would the government in Expatland take custody of the children for a period of time?

9. What is the level of estate taxes in Expatland?

10. Do you need insurance to fund estate taxes?

11. Can you make life-time gifts to lower the value of your estate?

12. If your Employment Visa in Expatland is supporting a dependent spouse, what is the process that your spouse would need to go through to remain in Expatland if desired?

13. What is the process for repatriating the deceased to the home country for burial or funeral services?

14. In terms of assets in Expatland, are there some that must be sold following your death or the relocation of your family from Expatland?

15. If your spouse returns to your home country with the children, what is the management plan for assets left in Expatland?

16. If you and your partner pre-decease your children, what age would you wish them to have full access to the capital?

17. Would you like to allow the children's guardian until they reach majority to have access to a portion of your estate to modify the guardian's home to comfortably accommodate your children?

18. Would you like the children's guardian to be remunerated for acting as guardian and, if so, on what basis – flat fee per annum or hourly rate?

19. Have you appointed outside experts to administer your Will and audit the estate to assist the guardian in their duties?

Exposure for Debts Post-Death

It is important to understand exposure for debts after a person has died. Usually the executor of the estate of the deceased is responsible for settling the deceased person's debts.

If a debt was solely in the name of the deceased, the executor can use the assets of the estate as either cash or selling assets to pay off the debt.

In rare cases, if the debts exceed the value of assets held in the name of the deceased, lenders will generally write off the sum.

However, you should be aware how the laws work in Expatland because it may be the case that under community property law, a debt taken on during a marriage can be considered community property, even if the debt was only in the name of the deceased.

Alternatively, the spouse or partner may have been a guarantor. In this case there is a need for the spouse or partner to have the ability to pay off the deceased's debt as the lender may pursue the spouse.

Being an authorised user on a credit card account generally does not mean you are liable for that debt if the cardholder dies; however, it may have the potential to cause some credit rating issues.

As a beneficiary under a Will you should be aware that generally creditors to the estate are first in line.

Selecting a Professional Estate Practitioner

It always makes sense to have a professional prepare your Will. Although some Will kits may promise that they have legal effect, there is always the possibility a mistake may be made that renders the Will invalid. The importance of reviewing and upgrading your existing Will cannot be overstated.

If you are unsure of how to select a professional, a good idea is to look at reputable global bodies such as the Society of Trust and Estate Practitioners (STEP) and obtain a recommendation. Other avenues are checking with private bankers, chartered accountants or CPAs.

Remember that although an estate plan can be expensive, the cost is immaterial when compared to having no Will or one that does not operate properly. Be clear that you understand what the fees will be, as some solicitors try to impose fees based on the percentage of assets of the estate.

When making a Will, consider the following top 10 points:

1. Settle all your valuable personal possessions and non-financial assets into a testamentary trust that arises on death. The reason for this is to avoid the potential for arguments among beneficiaries of your estate.

   If you have valuable personal items, it may be that future beneficiaries will argue about custody of those personal items and this will delay the granting of probate. What can also happen following death is that many personal possessions can go missing before probate starts.

   One option is to consider contributing all personal possessions into a testamentary trust and give trusteeship of that trust to an executor along with either an accountant or a lawyer. The terms of that trust could be to hold all your personal possessions and to give them complete discretion as to which beneficiary receives particular assets.

   A significant advantage of this approach is that it may prevent a probate judge delaying an estate administration while the potential beneficiaries argue with each other.

2. Consider using an insurance policy to top up your estate for second families. For those deceased who may have had second or third families, it may be that upon their demise, children from earlier marriages seek access to the assets.

This may be in spite of the fact that they were well provided for, educated and looked after prior to the subsequent marriage. In some parts of Expatland, all children will be treated equally, which can be unfair for subsequent children who may be more reliant on their parent's estate to be looked after in life.

To address this potential problem, an insurance top up can be implemented. With this solution, additional life insurance would be taken out directly in the name of the minor children or in the name of a trustee or guardian for the minor children.

As a directly held policy would not flow into the estate, adult children and other relatives would be unable to access these proceeds.

3. Understand the impact of taxes on the value of transferring assets. Simple Wills in which a spouse leaves all their assets to the other and vice versa before they have children or many assets often fail to consider the impact of estate taxes, which exist in many parts of Expatland, including the US and India.

   Many years later, when children arrive and there is more complexity in the individual balance sheet – the tax consequences of death can be significant.

   For example, a Will that requires an executor to sell an asset rather than transfer it in specie can trigger a capital gains tax bill that significantly reduces the amount available to a beneficiary. For example, many standard Will kits often do not contain sufficient flexibility in this regard. Although cost effective, standard Will Kits rarely provide a quality outcome and more often than not be invalid due to incorrect execution and/or witnessing rules in some countries.

Some tax systems have a provision that assets transferred following death do not give rise to a disposal and as such they will not be taxed.

Also your Will needs to allow for an executor to take the tax position of a beneficiary into account when considering a value transfer. Thus it may be that in the case of one beneficiary, a transfer of shares is better as there has been less gain or loss on the shares when compared to, say, other assets held by the estate.

4. Consider using professional co-executors to assist family members. Often married couples are the sole executors of their spouse's Will. This can pose a serious problem if one spouse becomes mentally incapacitated and no longer able to function in the role of executor. Co-executors or other executors that can take over if the first executor becomes of unsound mind can be crucial.

   In the absence of such arrangements, it may be that other family members would have to go to a court to have the executor declared mentally incompetent. In the case of testamentary trusts where the surviving spouse is the trustee of the trust, the same problem can exist. Using a public trust company or reputable accounting or law firm partner can be the solution.

   Concerns about having co-trustees can be addressed either by having an odd number of co-trustees providing that each trustee can act alone if they are of sound mind and are not acting fraudulently.

5. When using a testamentary or revocable trust ensure that the deed works properly and have it reviewed by a competent lawyer.

   If the assets of the testamentary trust are significant, then it is important to consider if the trustees have the skills necessary to operate and manage the trust. It may be that they do not have commercial or investment experience. In this case, the testamentary trust should allow the trustee to delegate investment advisory power to an external specialist.

   One important point to note here is that just because a trust may invest in a company, the trustees can still be obligated to monitor the activities of the company. For example, there are a number of trust cases where the trustee is the sole shareholder of a family company.

   In the event that the family company has an independent board of directors, it is simply not the case that the trustee can leave the running of the business to the board of directors.

   If there is a loss of value, the trustees may find themselves being sued for negligence.

   Consider the well-known English case of Bartlett v Barclays Bank. In that case Barclays Bank was the sole trustee of the Bartlett trust. The sole asset of the trust was 99.8 per cent of the issued shares in the family company. On the company board were two surveyors, an accountant and a solicitor. The trustee appointed none. In an attempt to raise cash, the trust appointed merchant bankers to consider taking the company public. The bankers advised that a public offering would be much more successful if the company expanded its business from managing property to developing property as well.

Barclays Bank as trustee agreed to this policy (so long as the income available to the beneficiaries was not affected). The board then embarked on speculative developments, one of which ended in disaster when planning permission could not be obtained for a large development (the Old Bailey project), and the trust suffered a significant loss.

Brightman J held that the bank, as trustee, had not discharged its duty as trustee in failing to supervise the new ventures of the company. He held that, given the size of the shareholding, the bank should have obtained the fullest information on the conduct of the business, and it was not sufficient to rely merely on the supply of information that they received in the ordinary course as a shareholder.

Their defence, that they honestly and reasonably believed the board of directors to be competent and capable of running the business, was rejected. The court reiterated older propositions as to the duty of trustees, "to conduct the business of the trust with the same care as an ordinary prudent man of business would extend to his own affairs".

However, the implication was that where a prudent person of business holds the majority of shares in a company, they would actively engage themselves in the company's undertakings rather than leaving it to the board.

In these cases, it is important for the trustee to make sure that the terms of the testamentary trust deed specifically protect them against this eventuality either by an appropriately drafted clause or by taking out material indemnity insurances.

Furthermore, depending upon the location within Expatland the existence of the trust may impose additional reporting obligations upon trustees. This would be the case where beneficiaries were US citizens, but the trust was located outside the US and indeed the trustees were not US persons.

6. Do some research to see if some of the assets owned can be transferred to a testamentary trust upon death. Some assets in Expatland may only be able to be held by nationals of that country. The expat may have had, for example, a complicated nominee and lease arrangement, which sometimes exists over real estate in Thailand and Vietnam.

   Merely assuming that a foreign executor and even an executor living in Expatland can take title of the deceased's assets is not a given. Similarly, it is important to consider if existing powers of attorney that were effective in your home country have relevance and operational ability in Expatland.

7. Out-of-date advanced healthcare directives need to be checked to see if the local laws of Expatland allow such a document to be executed. It may be that when you first arrived in Expatland the laws with respect to Advance Medical Directives recognised your home country Advance Medical Directives, but laws do change. Monitoring any changes in legislation is therefore very important.

In the US, for instance, if your advance healthcare directive was written before 2001, it will need to be revised to one that contains the current appropriate *Health and Insurance Portability and Accountability Act* (HIPAA) language.

Failure to check any legal changes may result in your nominated person being unable to, for example, gain access to your medical records or some other barrier to making an informed decision about your medical treatment.

Therefore, if some time has passed since you first executed your advance healthcare directive, then check that it contains all the necessary language and releases.

8. Leaving your pension life insurance policies direct to your spouse. In many cases pension plans hold life insurance policies. Upon death, insurance payouts under these policies often flow to a spouse.

   At a practical level, it makes sense to consider whether a spouse has liabilities. As such, insurance policies could be held in a 'spouse trust' whereby the spouse may benefit from income but defer receipt of capital.

   There are many reasons how or why a liability may arise. Some of these include:

   - Being a guarantor for the deceased's loans
   - Being liable as a director of business
   - Being a co-borrower with the deceased.

9. Improperly executed estate planning documents in the home country may need to be re-signed or validated in Expatland.

10. Failing to appoint guardians that can take immediate custody of the deceased's children. Most estate plans should include some provisions for guardians taking care of minor children. This is usually a relative or close friend of the deceased. While that is relatively straightforward in the home country, when expats move to Expatland this area needs great attention.

    A guardian who may reside in the home country may not be allowed into Expatland to act as guardian due to visa or other issues. Indeed the guardian's right to take custody of the children can also be delayed.

AT A GLANCE

- An estate plan is a document that considers what assets/ debts go where you want them to go.
- It is critical to have a good estate plan set up so that your assets and debts are handled smoothly.
- A useful starting point for expats with a Will in their home country is to make sure they are aware of the local legislation in Expatland.
- It makes sense to have a professional prepare your Will. Although some Will kits may promise that they have legal effect, a mistake could always be made that renders the Will invalid.
- When seeking the expertise of a professional, be clear that you understand what the fees will be as some solicitors try to impose fees based on the percentage of assets of the estate.
- Consider using professional co-executors to assist family members. It can also be crucial to have co-executors or other executors who can take over if the first executor becomes of unsound mind.
- If you have shares in a company or business, do you have a business succession plan?
- A Will needs to allow for an executor to take the tax position of a beneficiary into account when considering a value transfer.
- Having one executor who resides in the country where the deceased lived and worked can be worthwhile considering. At least a professional executor should be appointed as a

co-executor to assist in the management and divestment of property under an expat's Will.

- It is advisable to have a letter of instruction that can provide a list of instructions for people to follow, such as where your Will may be found.
- Make sure your accountant or financial advisor has an up-to-date listing of your assets.
- Have a list of all organisations in which you are a member, as some of these may provide death benefits as part of the membership. Generally creditors to the estate are first in line, not the beneficiaries.
- Do you have family members, such as your siblings, whom you wish to receive more benefit from your estate than others? You need to explore what the rules are for covering this type of favouritism in Expatland.
- It is important to understand exposure for debts after a person has passed away in Expatland.
- You may wish to have a living Will in the event that you lapse into a comatose state and are unable to make your own decisions.
- Settling all your valuable personal possessions and non-financial assets into a testamentary trust that arises on death will prevent arguments among beneficiaries of your estate.
- Simple Wills in which a spouse leaves all their assets to the other and vice versa before they have children or many assets often fail to consider the impact of estate taxes.

8

EXPATLAND INSURANCE

For most new expats arriving in Expatland, the word 'insurance' means many different things. It can cover life insurance; property insurance; home and contents insurance; medical and critical illness insurance; and income protection insurance.

Insurance is designed to provide peace of mind, but it is only as good as the benefits it can provide and the legal terms and conditions stated in the contract.

Medical Insurance & Healthcare

One of the many challenges when leaving your home country for Expatland is the issue of healthcare. For those on a traditional 'expat package', finding quality co-ordinated healthcare is the key here.

If the employer provides the cost of the medical insurance, then the financial implications are not the main issue.

However, for an expat on a 'local package' or for an expat who is self-employed, the financial implications of expat healthcare can be astronomical.

The following are some key questions of material significance to the expat in Expatland:

1. How do you implement your primary health coverage?

2. If you need to return to your home country for specialised treatment, how does the 'health parachute' work?

3. If you remain covered by a home country Medicare system, would this still apply for those periods of time you return to your home country?

4. What are the key things to consider when reviewing a health policy in your home country?

5. If you are in a less developed country, do you need an air ambulance insurance policy?

6. Do you need to prepare a local healthcare directive? A healthcare directive is a document that lets others know about your wishes with respect to your healthcare. It is a legal document that allows you to appoint a person to decide for you if you're not able to make decisions for yourself.

7. Do your family members back home understand what you want to do if you become incapacitated?

A number of these challenges are related to your age, your location in Expatland, your current insurance and financial position. However, you should have a healthcare strategy in place while you are in Expatland.

It is vital to understand the standard and type of healthcare available to you and your family in Expatland. This is particularly the case if you are travelling to Expatland with a pre-existing medical condition.

If the pre-existing medical condition requires ongoing care, then considering how much this will cost and who will provide the level of care in Expatland is essential.

While most countries do have a given level of basic healthcare programs and facilities, it may be the case that some of the more advanced treatments and procedures may not exist in your Expatland location.

If this seems likely, then obtaining global medical coverage from a reputable provider is essential. It is important to find out that, if needed, you can travel to another third country location and remain insured. Not only would the cost of the treatment in the third country be a requirement, but ideally any travel costs would also need to be covered.

Recently one of our expat clients suffered the misfortune of having their teenage child severely injured while holidaying in an Asian location. Although outside their home country or their arrival country – the expat client's insurance policy covered all members of the family not only for direct medical costs but also the costs of transporting the teenager to Australia. The teenager was able to obtain hundreds of thousands of dollars of medical attention under the policy and will continue rehabilitation for a number of years under the policy. This provided enormous peace of mind to the distraught parents.

In a number of countries the cost of healthcare is significant, such as in the US. While an expat may have cover as an employee, does that cover extend to family members as well as the employee for a certain period following loss of employment?

While public hospitals in some Expatland locations may be free of charge, the level of care may not be up to your standards. For this reason private medical healthcare insurance is essential in Expatland.

When implementing your health insurance, it is important to check factors such as whether there are exclusions preventing coverage from certain illnesses that may be likely to affect you or whether you have to use a certain range of healthcare service providers. We have already discussed that it is important to check that the policy should cover you for emergency evacuation in the event you need medical treatment.

Before arriving in Expatland, it is worth commencing your search for a good doctor. A good way of finding one is to ask for recommendations.

Of equal importance before you arrive is to understand what inoculations or health certificates are needed for entry and what the requirements of the local vaccination program are.

A number of diseases such as dengue fever, typhoid or cholera are prevalent in many locations within Expatland. It is important to note that the risk of infection often varies between the city and countryside. Prior to your move, make sure you enquire about any specific health risks in Expatland.

While there are a number of websites that list diseases prevalent in a number of countries (see the World Health Organization:

http://www.who.int/en/), it is best on local health issues to seek advice from doctors or other health professionals in Expatland rather than in your home country.

How to Choose Medical Cover

A useful starting point for choosing medical cover might be to look at the policy you had in your home country. You should also define your needs and those of your family.

Check with your doctor and other healthcare professionals for current prescriptions before you leave your home country and make sure you take along enough medical supplies that you and your family need. This is particularly the case with prescription medicines, as they may not be commonly available at your destination.

In some locations in Expatland, even common drugs routinely available in your home country may be unavailable. There can also be the issue of different names being used for similar underlying health issues. It is important to take extra care in choosing the right medication upon arrival in Expatland.

There are a wide variety of insurance service providers and they vary significantly from country to country. It may be that your employer organisation has a list of preferred medical service providers that are offered as part of your corporate medical insurance program. Alternatively, you may be free to choose your own doctor and have this covered by your employer or healthfund medical provider.

In many locations in Expatland, it is not possible to see a medical specialist without a referral from a general practitioner (as is the case in Australia).

Dental care in Expatland is also a matter of research and study. If the location in Expatland does not have a sound history of dental services, you may find yourself at the mercy of sub-standard dentists or orthodontists. It is imperative that your medical cover allows you to travel to a third country to obtain professional dental services.

It is important, however, to have private medical insurance, because when choosing your own medical service provider costs can mount up. Additionally, elective surgery waiting lists can be very long.

Expats who go to work in other locations in Expatland, like Singapore, may have the option of a corporate healthcare scheme that would generally cover themselves and their families.

By contrast, other countries such as Denmark do not provide access to public health services until registration, so having private cover is essential. Furthermore, those expats travelling to other locations in Expatland may find that the location offers a 'no insurance, no visa' policy.

Given the emergence of globally based corporations combined with improvements in communication there are a vast range of health insurance companies offering their services internationally.

The market for these services is growing significantly and suppliers are rushing to fill the void and offering more and more professional plans.

However, of the estimated 230 million expats in Expatland, less than 50 per cent of these hold valid health insurance plans. Many expats assume that the plans they left home will still apply while they live overseas.

It is not our purpose here to nominate healthcare providers, but some research will yield readily available service providers.

For new arrivals to Expatland, it is sometimes a shock to the system to realise that medical treatment of an acceptable standard is either not available or otherwise much more expensive. Conditions vary widely through Expatland.

In some parts of Expatland, the promotion of medical insurance plans is done via a global network of specialist brokers and independent financial advisors.

In other cases this occurs via the plan insurers themselves, but we always recommend obtaining independent specialist advice for the following reasons:

- This is more likely to ensure that you buy the right plan for your circumstances;
- The cost of the premiums are appropriate for the country; and
- Any hidden costs and commissions are more likely to be identified by an external party assisting you.

If you are not comfortable reading legal documentation, then have your solicitor review the policy wording, exclusions and areas of uncertainty.

Given the multitude of other issues you will have to deal with, implementing insurance is sometimes done in haste. However, a trap for the unwary is to incorrectly complete the application form. An insurance company can deny a claim on the basis of an incorrectly completed application form, so this is an area you need to pay particular attention to.

The cost of private healthcare is important, but given the actuarial basis for calculation of insurance premiums there is usually a good reason why a policy is cheaper. It is more likely so because of the exclusions in the policy, reducing the likelihood that a claim will be paid out. For example, contracting dengue fever while trekking in the highlands for Borneo may be excluded!

It is better to know about the exclusions before you undertake vetoed activities for travel to excluded coverage areas.

Other traps to watch for are 'capped cover policies' or policies requiring a high 'excess' before the policy claim can be paid out. What may seem like a generous cap in one location may soon be exceeded in another.

Premiums should be the 'last' thing looked at when comparing policies.

Key Definitions in Medical Plans

Generally speaking, when implementing medical insurance you need to decide if your application will be a full underwriting or moratorium application.

A full underwriting plan process will usually require input from medical practitioners who have attended to you in the past. Letters and other documents confirming your medical history are generally required. This is so that specific conditions may be covered or indeed that certain conditions (such as HIV) are covered at all.

In a full underwriting application all that you will be required to do is to complete medical history questions. Once the potential insurer understands your medical history they may, depending upon your state of health, exclude certain conditions from cover.

Unlike a full underwriting plan, a moratorium plan generally provides that pre-existing conditions, which have resulted in treatment within a defined time frame, are excluded from cover.

In these policies, if no further treatment is required again within a given time frame, then some insurers will add this condition to your policy cover.

In Appendix C, 'Key Questions for Health Insurance Providers & Websites', we set out for your review some key questions to ask your proposed insurance provider, as well as some helpful websites to assist in your research.

Medical Plan Structures

While many international plans have different titles to do with branding and marketing, the reality is that global insurance plans usually have three key components. These are:

- Inpatient or daycare treatment
- Outpatient treatment
- Additional add-on options.

A normal plan will generally include in-patient and daycare treatment. No outpatient or other cover is provided under these types of plans.

More comprehensive plans will cover outpatient treatment in addition to the inpatient costs. Usually these will have a capped limit.

Finally, the top-of-the-line plans will generally offer the complete range of in-patient, daycare and outpatient. Also routine dental care will be included together with other types of cover, such as personal accident or maternity cover.

Of central importance when comparing plans is to make sure you are comparing like with like. You need to make sure that you have a clear understanding of benefits, areas of cover, exclusions and caps.

For example, an Australian expat living in Rome who never needs cover in Australia apart from the occasional holiday trip, could opt for Area 1 European cover, which costs much less than full, worldwide cover. (Area 2 generally refers to "worldwide cover excluding the US or Canada" while Area 3 is the most expensive as it offers full global cover including the US.)

Certain insurers will offer discrete benefit options where clients have the ability to select features and hence calculate their own premiums.

Disaster Planning

In the event that life throws a curve ball, there are some crucial questions to ask. Does your health plan include evacuation and repatriation options? For instance, in the event of the death of a policyholder, are the costs of moving the mortal remains covered or is that an add-on benefit?

It is essential to understand what is included in any evacuation or repatriation cover. In one case, an expat client of mine discovered that his plan covered only the travel cost and not any accommodation. Information like this will not seem important until it is actually needed. Your plan should also cover return trips to the point of your first departure.

Another key question to ask is whether the plan allows for another person to accompany you when you are being evacuated for treatment?

There have been many instances of emergency treatment while being abroad, which is not only stressful but also expensive. If you are able to be accompanied, it is a huge advantage.

Doctor Costs/Outpatient Expenses

Most expats with families know that before arriving in Expatland costs of seeing a doctor and other outpatient costs, such as pharmacy expenses, are usually the main healthcare cost when at home. It is even more likely that this will continue to be the case in Expatland.

For those expats located in developing parts of Expatland, children are much more likely to need regular medical services – and even adults can be more susceptible to illness in hotter climates.

Determining how visits to the doctor will be treated under your policy is essential. Ask if those costs will be fully or only partly reimbursed and what is the applicable excess for doctor visits.

You need to make sure that you review the health plan carefully as most insurers will limit outpatient benefits to contain cost. These restrictions should be studied carefully in the plan. Also examine the wording carefully concerning whether medication is capped financially or not. Some plans will offer "elective" or "well woman/ well man" checks, meaning that preventive costs for just a check-up can be covered.

Other providers will not reimburse for this type of expense, but will wait to reimburse expenses only after you are ill and have visited a doctor. This is an important area worthy of clarification.

Other Add-on Options

Depending upon affordability, it may be worth adding further options to your medical plan. Outpatient and inpatient/daycare cover makes sense, because while in-patient care will provide catastrophic or hospital cost cover, it will not cover you if you are 'walking wounded'.

Another add-on is for elective dental – while most plans will cover accidental damage to your teeth, they will exclude elective dental healthcare.

While routine dental treatment is usually quoted strangely as an "optional extra", how can dental cover be considered optional? This would not cover costs such as visiting the dentist for a crown. Usually you would have to pay this expense on most plans.

Maternity cover is also important as experience shows that many families are unprepared and only contact their healthcare broker when their baby is on the way! If you are thinking of starting a family in Expatland it's best that you take insurance cover before your pregnancy. Otherwise this is an exclusion in most policies, as almost all insurers will view an existing pregnancy as a pre-existing condition.

Summary

Purchasing a full coverage healthcare plan from a reputable insurer through an experienced independent broker is usually the correct way of proceeding. If, however, you go for cost alone and you do not take proper independent advice, disappointment is likely to be around the corner.

Exclusions are there for a reason and are directly related to the price of the insurance plan. Beware of the fineprint and make sure you understand the terms and conditions very well, being mindful that you are also selecting the correct type of health plan for your geographical area.

As with all insurance, international expat medical insurance is about peace of mind. If cost is a stumbling block, premiums can be reduced by accepting higher excess on claims, which will make quality insurance products more affordable.

My view is that you should at a minimum study three insurers across a number of key performance indicators outlined in this section.

Even those on the full expat package sometimes find that the degree of coverage with respect to particular services, such as general dentistry and orthodontal, do not provide sufficient levels of cover to equate with the benefits that were previously accessible in the home country.

For expats moving on a local package – which is a package that treats the expats as any other local in Expatland – failing to calculate the cost of health for family and children is often an expensive mistake. It can have a negative impact if there are pre-existing health conditions and the medical policy on offer excludes some particular condition.

It is therefore advisable to obtain an international healthcare policy from providers such as global healthcare companies to cover you and your family in defined hospitals in certain parts of Expatland. This will avoid putting yourself in the position of leaving your family exposed if a health incident occurs.

Further below I will examine other forms of insurance, but much of what has been said with respect to medical insurance will also have application for other types of insurance.

Advanced Healthcare Directives

Depending upon your location in Expatland, you need to know the law around advanced healthcare directives.

As noted earlier an 'advance healthcare directive' lets your doctor, family and friends know your healthcare preferences. This includes the types of special treatment you wish to have or not have at the end of life, your desire for diagnostic testing, surgical procedures, resuscitation and any organ donation.

By planning your options early, you can ensure the quality of life that is important to you and avoid having your family 'guess' your wishes or having to make critical medical care decisions for you when they are under stress or in an emotional state.

Checklist

This checklist for advanced healthcare directives can be very helpful in avoiding unnecessary stress to your family:

1. **Collect relevant information for decision-making.** Your doctor is a good place to start for understanding your options on healthcare treatment at the end of life. In addition, many organisations have information that may be useful.

2. **Discuss your end-of-life decisions with relevant people.** Talk about your decisions with your family, physician and others who are close to you. Questions to consider for discussion are:

    - What is important to you when you are dying?

    - Are there specific medical treatments you especially want or do not want?

    - When you are dying, do you want to be in a nursing home, hospital or at home?

    - What are the options in palliative care/pain management and hospice care?

3. **Prepare your advance care directive form.** Under the relevant law, find out if you have a legal right to express your healthcare wishes when you are unable to make these decisions yourself. It is advisable to nominate a person to handle your healthcare choices, making sure you discuss the matter with them. You could name a spouse, relative or other agent.

After you have selected the person and they have agreed to act in this capacity, then inform key people of your end-of-life preferences, such as your doctor, family and close friends.

Keep a copy of your signed and completed advance healthcare directive safe and accessible. This will help ensure that your wishes will be known at the critical time and carried out. It is wise to also give a copy of your form to the person you appoint as your agent and any alternate designated agents. Give a copy to your doctor; healthcare providers; the healthcare institution that is providing your care (if known in advance); family members; and any other responsible person who is likely to be called if there is a medical emergency.

Moving to Expatland has an impact on both general and personal insurances and it is important to consider these insurances, such as life, income protection and total and permanent disability cover.

Each of these insurance types are designed to cover different events.

For example, life insurance generally provides a lump sum in the event of death or diagnosis of a major illness. This is a key area of concern – life insurance if it has an investment component may result in some tax exposure in Expatland. This is worth further analysis, as expats generally don't consider an insurance product in a foreign country as exposing them to a tax liability in Expatland.

In the case of income protection insurance, it mostly provides a certain percentage of your usual income if you are no longer able to work due to ill health or employment redundancy.

In the case of total and permanent disability, it provides a lump sum for this event. For a trauma or critical illness policy, this type of cover generally provides a lump sum on the diagnosis of a range of illnesses. While the function of this section is not to discuss the policy in detail, it's important to recognise that moving to Expatland can actually render some of these policies null and void.

An example of this may be income protection where coverage is only provided under the policy if the income being protected is derived in the home country. In the case of life insurance, it may be that moving to a high-risk jurisdiction renders the policy null and void.

It's important that if insurance is in place, that it is not rendered invalid by moving to Expatland. Many expats do not consider the impact of moving to Expatland until after they have arrived – and in some cases that is too late. The reason why it can be too late is that some policies have a clause in them (income protection policies as an example) that after 12 months of living overseas the home country policy lapses. In that case if you have had a decline in the standard of your health you may not be able to be insured in Expatland.

So it is important that you carefully examine the wording of your policies. Consult the insurance agent, and where possible enter into new policies to cover risks that may cease being covered simply by your move to Expatland.

The degree to which the insurance market is developed in Expatland also needs to be thought about. In most major parts of Expatland the insurance industry has existed for a number of years, but in some countries the policies are not guaranteed to be renewable. There may also be difficulties in prosecuting a claim in the event of illness or accident.

A major part of any move to Expatland requires thorough scrutiny of how existing personal insurance policies for your expat spouse and children are impacted.

Other types of insurance, such as general insurance, also need consideration.

General Insurance

General insurance typically covers household contents, artwork and other personal possessions. While the relocation company chosen to move your goods to your new Expatland residence should cover the goods to the point of delivery, there needs to be a policy in place to cover the value of the goods and personal possessions after delivery.

Again you need to study the legal system of Expatland so that a general insurance of comparable or better quality can be put in place.

There was a case of an expat client who, having moved a piece of art to Expatland, suffered a theft. Unfortunately, he discovered that his failure to list that artwork meant that it was not covered by the insurance. These are traps for any unwary expats, and it best to make sure that valuable items are listed and identified and also appropriate insurance is put in place by the time the items leave the care of the global relocation company.

AT A GLANCE

- Good healthcare is essential in Expatland. Research your options carefully, ensuring your spouse and children are adequately covered.
- When looking for a healthfund, first define your needs and those of your family.
- Understand what the standard and type of healthcare is available to you and your family in Expatland, particularly in the case of pre-existing conditions.
- Check that your healthfund covers travel to a third country location.
- Check if there are exclusions preventing coverage from certain illnesses.
- Bring to Expatland enough supplies of any medicines or prescriptions that are needed by you or your family.
- When comparing plans, make sure you are comparing 'apples with apples'.
- Does your health plan include evacuation and repatriation options, including accommodation costs? Does it cover someone accompanying you if repatriation is needed and you can't travel alone?
- Purchasing a full coverage healthcare plan from a reputable insurer through an experienced independent broker is advisable.
- An 'advance healthcare directive' lets your doctor, family and friends know your healthcare preferences in case of a terminal event.

- A major part of any move to Expatland requires a thorough examination of your existing general insurance policies, such as life insurance and home and contents. Make sure these are updated to cover living in Expatland.
- If a policy was implemented in your home country, consider whether the insurance policy with an underlying assets element results in taxation exposure in the arrival country.
- Fill out your healthfund application form carefully. An insurance company can deny a claim on the basis of an incorrectly completed application form.
- Find a good doctor in Expatland before you need one. Ask for recommendations from fellow expats.
- Be wary of a cheap healthfund policy. There is likely to be exclusions in the policy, reducing the likelihood that a claim will be paid out.
- If your partner is of child-bearing age, make sure you have maternity cover before the event.

9

EXPATLAND LEGAL

As was the case in relation to tax considerations to think through before your move to Expatland, there are four key questions that should be asked when considering moving to Expatland.

The first would include questions about the legal system, covering the following:

- What is the legal system that applies in the country that I am moving to?
- Is it a civil or common law jurisdiction?
- Or is it a hybrid legal system?
- What are your basic legal rights in relation to the part of Expatland you are moving to?

Common Law Regime

In the US, a common law regime is a body of unwritten laws based on precedents established by the courts. Common law is used in deciding novel cases where the outcome cannot be determined based on existing statutes. The US common law system evolved from the pre-colonial system of English common law. The decisions

(precedents) of higher courts are binding on lower courts so that the US legal system will have consistency and stability. However, lower courts can choose to modify precedent or distinguish from precedent if precedents are outdated or if the current case is substantially different from the precedent case. Lower courts can also choose to overturn precedent, but this is rare.

Common law is developed by judges through court decisions similar to tribunals, as opposed to statutes adopted through the legislative process or regulations issued by the executive branch.

A common law regime is a regime that relies on precedents to provide guidance on subsequent court cases on the basis that it is unfair to treat similar facts differently on different occasions.

The body of legal precedents called 'common law' effectively binds future decisions. In cases where the parties disagree on what the law is, a common law court will refer to prior court cases from the relevant court to consider decisions that might apply to the matter at hand.

If a current legal dispute has been resolved in the past, the court is usually bound to follow the reasoning used in the prior decision.

The common law system, as developed in the UK, forms the basis of Australian jurisprudence. It is distinct from the civil law systems that operate in Europe, South America and Japan, which are derived from Roman law. Other countries that employ variations of the common law system are the US, Canada, New Zealand, Malaysia and India.

Civil Law Regime

The countries of Europe, Latin America and many parts of the world operate under such a system. The civil law system derives from Roman law.

The history of civil law as established under Roman law relates to the rules and principles of private law compiled in the *Corpus Juris Civilis* as propounded by the Emperor Justinian in the 6th century.

The *Corpus Juris Civilis* contained a list of earlier legal writings and an explanation of earlier Roman law together with a new body of rules introduced by Justinian.

Corpus Juris Civilis also included the Institutes, which set out the private law. This law became the basis for the French Code Napoleon of 1807, which was the model for codes implemented through continental Europe and Latin America.

Hybrid Legal Regime

A hybrid legal system refers to a legal system that utilises both common law and civil law in the administration of its justice system. An example of such a country is Mauritius.

In Mauritius the legal system operates using a hybrid legal system based on English and French law. The law relating to criminal and civil litigation procedures is mainly English while the main bodies of substantial law are based on the civil law of the French Napoleonic code. Company law is based on the common law of England and New Zealand.

Mauritius also has a wide range of double tax agreements.

The reason why it is important to understand the basic structure of the legal systems is that the nature of any disputes that may occur when you or your family are in that country are very important to recognise.

For example, does the jurisdiction recognise the law of superior courts or foreign courts? For instance, some countries that are common law countries – such as New Zealand and Australia – did for many years allow an appeal to the Privy Council in England if a decision of the Court of the relevant country was not acceptable to one of the litigants. Also given the existence of 'common law', while foreign decisions may not be legally binding they can be cited as a relevant authority by the court of another jurisdiction in arriving at a court decision.

Some Middle Eastern countries still operate what may be referred to as 'debtor prisons'. People who suffer financial difficulties or owe money can be incarcerated in these debtor prisons because they owe funds to another party and it is a commercial dispute. In a recent case, executives of an Australian property group were held in the United Arab Emirate because of a legal dispute involving an Australian company. This is a significant point to understand before moving to a country. (Please refer to the article in Appendix D, 'Foreign Legal Systems'.)

For instance, if you have entered a country on an employment visa, what are the category of offences that may occur, ranging from traffic offences to more serious ones, that can result in your employment visa being cancelled and having to leave the country with little or no warning.

Some countries in Asia have a very harsh legal system when it comes to certain social behaviour that may otherwise be accepted in other countries. Some countries allow such behaviour as drinking alcohol, while other countries do not.

So a general overview and understanding of the laws of the country where you will be living as well as how they may impact upon you and your family are very important.

The second question to consider is what are the consequences of being involved in a commercial dispute in the country of arrival. Find out whether or not there is suitable employment law and how it operates, or whether litigation can be commenced against an employer or business partner who fails to honour their obligations.

Thirdly, from an estate planning perspective, find out how the laws of inheritance and deceased estates work in the country you are arriving in. For example, does a foreign Will have validity in the country should an unfortunate death occur and how would your estate plan be impacted if this is not the case?

Fourthly, do you need a power of attorney in the country of arrival such that a spouse can sign on your behalf and vice versa if you lose consciousness or mental capacity?

If it is not the case, does a foreign power of attorney need to be prepared in the arrival country? You also need to understand other disclosure obligations in respect to foreign assets unrelated to income tax that may exist.

Finally, should you happen to divorce in the country, what are the consequences in terms of custody of children and how do those laws operate?

I recall a case where a client, upon separating from her partner in a Middle Eastern country, was unable to secure custody of her children.

Another example of these considerations is if your potential heirs or beneficiaries are US citizens, you may be considering the trade-off between a stringent US gift and estate tax against a worse outcome of inheritance taxes.

Under the code, a US citizen, resident or trust receiving a gift or device from an expatriate is subject to an inheritance tax at the highest applicable gift or estate tax rate; planning therefore needs to be done in these areas.

We also need to consider that laws in some countries could cancel or void inheritance plans that are structured to give an intended though harsh treatment to a beneficiary under a Will. For example, in some countries disinheriting a child is not possible. It may be possible to state in your Will that the law of a foreign jurisdiction should apply to your estate.

Estate taxes in your arrival country may be higher than your home country. Another question to ask yourself is whether the employment agreement that you are employed under – together with any bonuses agreements or other agreements – are legal in the country that you have expatriated to.

As an example, let us consider the case of one of our expatriate banking clients who, in 2008, entered into an employment agreement with a major investment bank offering a guaranteed bonus in the US. Following the financial crisis US regulators announced rules with respect to bank pay and remuneration arrangements that changed the existing deal the employee had with his bank employer.

There are usually four ways an expatriate assignment can be set up and you need to work out if your employment agreement is to be regarded as a secondment employment by the foreign office, localisation, transfer or whether you are working in fact for both home and host countries. Other legal issues to consider are the impact of accessing foreign pension or superannuation plans when you are in the arrival country.

AT A GLANCE

- Find out what legal system is being used in your location in Expatland.
- Find out what are the category of offences that may occur – from a traffic offence to something more serious – that can result in your employment visa being cancelled.
- Find out what are the consequences of being involved in some sort of commercial or business dispute.
- Learn how the laws of inheritance and deceased estates work in Expatland.
- Investigate the operation of a power of attorney. Do you need a power of attorney in the country of arrival such that a spouse can sign on your behalf and vice versa if you lose consciousness or mental capacity.
- Consider any disclosure obligations in respect of foreign assets.
- Don't move to Expatland without understanding if there is a double tax agreement in place between your home country and your arrival country.
- The divorce laws may not be the same as in your home country. The terms of custody of children may be extremely different, for example.
- Make yourself familiar with details of pensions or superannuation plans. Accessing these may be complicated in your arrival country.
- Retain all your tax records for the relevant retention period after you have moved to Expatland.

- Check what the consequences are for having children in Expatland, especially in relationship to National Service obligations or other ramifications.

10

EXPATLAND MORTGAGES

When you move to Expatland, your mortgage also goes with you. Keep in mind that there are banks in Expatland that will often be able to refinance your home country loan at a better rate.

For example, you may own real estate in the UK, France, Australia or the US, and the interest rate and the terms of the loan on offer in your home country may not be as advantageous as a loan from an Expatland financial institution.

Take an Australian home loan, for example – presently the interest rates on Australian dollar mortgages on a variable loan basis can be 1 per cent cheaper in, let's say, Hong Kong or Singapore when compared to a bank in Australia. It is important to know that you have the option of moving your mortgage along with yourself to Expatland!

You can also borrow funds in a foreign currency – if you have a mortgage on a house in Australia that mortgage could be refinanced in Expatland and converted to a US loan, or a Singapore or Hong Kong dollar loan. In some circumstances, the interest rate would be less than the equivalent Australian dollar loan.

However, a word of caution: Lower interest rates usually mean foreign currency risk if your property is in one currency and your

loan is in another currency. So you would need to be comfortable that your security – your real estate – is not exposed if there is an adverse foreign exchange rate movement.

We have seen situations where expats have used a foreign currency loan to finance their property in their home country and although the interest savings are attractive they have been left out of pocket when there was an adverse currency movement. In one particular case the expat owed the bank more money than their house was worth.

Consider the following example:

Expat Moving from Australia to Hong Kong

Assume an expat's house is worth AUD$2m when they leave Australia bound for Hong Kong. Also assume they have a mortgage of AUD$1.2m on the same property.

Upon discovering that HKD interest rates are 1 per cent, the expat is keen to move their mortgage into HKD. Hence on the day of the refinance – the AUD$1.2m converts to HKD$7.2m assuming an exchange rate of AUD$1 = HKD$6. This seems fine because the Australian property is also worth HKD$12m.

Bear in mind, though, that the expat has committed to repaying the bank in HKD the amount of HKD$7.2m.

The expat is vulnerable in this case to currency movement, which may affect the security position of the bank.

Let us assume now that the Australian dollar weakens heavily against the Hong Kong dollar – such that AUD$1 = HKD$4.

In effect this means that the security the bank is holding is now only worth HKD$8m down from HKD$12m. This happened purely due to exchange rate movements.

The bank is now in a position where they are owed HKD$7.2m but their security is only HKD$8m. Their security position has diminished from 60 per cent Loan to Value Ratio ('LVR') (that is debt of HKD$7.2m on a property worth HKD$12m) to 90 per cent LVR (that is the debt of HKD$7.2m on property now worth HKD$8m).

In this case the bank would be expected to ask the expat to send them additional funds to bring the Loan to Value Ratio either to 60 per cent or to a level the bank will accept. In this case the amount of HKD needed to bring the LVR down to 60 per cent would be HKD$2,400,000.

This would not be a pleasant experience if the expat is unprepared. Hence beware of cheap interest rates and how you might use them to finance foreign assets such as real estate.

From our experience, what a number of expats have done is to move the mortgage and keep much of the borrowing in their home currency. They potentially use foreign currency to refinance a small portion of the debt; this is done in times of high interest rates in their home country to perhaps lessen the overall impact of high interest rates.

It is important that you check to see that the terms and conditions of the mortgage in the new country are comparable to those in the home country. Other laws relating to consumer protection enforcement of a loan against the security need to be understood as well as the roll-over and repayment terms. However, re-mortgaging your home country property in Expatland is something that many expats have done correctly. This can offer a greater level of freedom and flexibility.

Some expats are tempted by the easy credit to borrow and buy new real estate in the country of arrival. While this is tempting, you need to be cautious for a number of reasons.

The dynamics of the property market in Expatland may not be the same as your home market, and taxation with respect to holding real estate may be higher or lower than in the home country.

The market may also operate in a way not based on supply and demand; for instance, certain countries in Asia use government techniques to artificially manage their property markets. They do this by directing banks to change their lending practices, potentially imposing higher or lower property taxes or alternatively requiring greater legal approval to buy new property – all of which affects the price of existing property.

Buying property in Expatland has to be undertaken with caution and only after a number of threshold questions have been understood and you have researched the possibility carefully.

A key consideration is that if you have to leave Expatland sooner than you intended, it may not be an opportune time to sell your real estate. The property may have been suitable for you to live in, but not good as a rental property. Holding it and managing it from your home country may also be difficult, and finally the tax consequences in your home country from deriving rental income in Expatland may make it less attractive to hold the property.

In one case we had an expat client who owned 'landed property' in Singapore. Essentially this means real estate upon which sits a freestanding house. The expat client was requested by their employer to leave Singapore and take up an assignment in another country. Given the particular requirements of Singapore, the expat client was under a legal requirement to sell their property.

This obligation could have caused them significant tax exposure in the country that the expat client was moving to. Furthermore, as the expat client had to sell the real estate at a time not of his choosing the market for real estate was depressed. In this case considerable planning time was needed to mitigate tax costs of him selling the real estate and moving to the new country.

AT A GLANCE

- Consider whether Expatland banks may be able to refinance your home country loan at a better rate than in your home country.
- Carefully examine the risks of borrowing funds in a foreign currency.
- Consult with real estate specialists, valuers and lawyers before buying real estate in Expatland as the dynamics of the property market in Expatland may not be the same as the home market.
- Consider that the level of taxation with respect to holding real estate may be higher or lower than your home country.
- Do not buy real estate without considering what would happen if you had to leave Expatland sooner than you intended.
- Mortgage terms and conditions may not be the same as those in your home country.
- First extensively research taking out loans and buying new real estate in the country of arrival.
- Don't forget to check whether you can obtain mortgage insurance to protect you in case you are unable to pay your mortgage.

11

EXPATLAND SECURITY

Expatland offers many diverse living environments. From parts of Expatland such as Singapore, which is one of the safest countries in the world, to other well-known, high-risk jurisdictions like Mexico City, there is great variability in planning for your security and that of your family.

Be Prepared

The Boy Scout's motto of 'be prepared' is the best advice. It is advisable to assess your part of Expatland and understand the risks clearly before arrival.

The range of threats to your personal safety will be higher in some places. For example, it is not uncommon for some of our clients to have 'bodyguards' escorting their children to school in parts of Latin America and the Middle East.

It is about a sense of proportion. Other threats to your physical safety can vary from planned robberies to random assaults.

In parts of Africa and the Middle East, seemingly innocuous activities take on a much higher degree of risk. A woman walking alone through a market is a non-event in Hong Kong, but in other parts of Expatland this could present a serious security risk.

The Groundwork

Preparing for potential outcomes often ensures that in the event of a threat or a dangerous situation presenting itself you have a plan of action.

When planning emergency strategies, make sure that you know who the relevant people are, such as fire, police and other emergency services personnel, and how to contact them quickly.

Keep duplicate copies of key documents such as birth certificates, passports, insurances and bank details in a safe but accessible place for the family. Also make sure that your home country advisors and family members know how to access your important information online or elsewhere as needed.

Travelling Safety

When leaving your home country, make sure that you have read all government travel advisories and that you are aware of the political and security situation in your part of Expatland.

A number of clients going to Japan changed their plans following the 2011 tsunami and subsequent nuclear accident. Other clients returned to their home country sooner than they otherwise would have due to this disaster.

Random protests can quickly turn into national disputes as we have seen in some South-East Asian countries, such as Thailand. Being an expat at times like this carries additional risk. However, no move to Expatland is entirely without risk, but in the vast majority of cases the benefits outweigh the risks.

Here are some key points that will help make your Expatland adventure safer:

- At airport terminals, be cautious about strangers who are overly friendly. In a recent case, one of my clients had their passport stolen at a major European airport. They not only missed their flight, but they had to spend 72 hours in the airport before being released.

- Always be aware of your surroundings. After a long flight there is a temptation to turn off or relax upon landing. However, this can often be the time when unsuspecting travellers are taken advantage of because they are jet-lagged or unfamiliar in their new surroundings. When you are moving from the terminal to the taxi stand or hire car, make sure your family are around you and luggage is secure and accounted for. Often a distraction can be created to divert your attention at this point.

- If you are driving in a new country, always get a GPS and/or if possible make sure you have someone to meet you and show you the way to your hotel.

- When travelling in Expatland or on holidays, never leave your kids alone or with people you are not very well acquainted with. There have been tragic stories of expats who have had their children kidnapped and never seen again.

- Remember that you are not a local and there may be a lot going on that could take a while to adjust to.

Assess the Risk

In some parts of Expatland, employing home help is normal. However, make sure they come from a reputable service and have permission to be working in Expatland. It is wise to keep an easily accessible file containing a copy of their passport and other details just in case you need to refer to them later.

Before installing security like 'nanny cams', check the Expatland law, as some devices like these are not legal in many countries. In any event, you might consider having a home safe in which to keep valuables and other prized pieces of jewellery, watches and other keepsakes.

Home & Surrounds Safety

Take some time to learn about the area you are going to live in and its history. Find out as much as you can about the physical environment, such as proximity to police, the fire brigade, hospital and ambulance. It's also a good idea to learn all the different ways in and out of the area *before* you sign a lease. If there is a church, temple or other religious building nearby, where there are often large numbers of unknown people moving around, ease of access in and out of your property could present security problems.

Try and understand the ethnic makeup of the area you will be living in. In some Middle Eastern countries, expat compounds are the standard. In other countries, expats live among people from all walks of life. It's not a bad idea to have a good chat with local shopkeepers and business owners before moving in. Don't just accept the statements of the real estate letting agent.

School Location

If you are selecting local schools for your children in Expatland, there will usually be ample reference points to check about safety within the school. However, remember to also acquaint yourself with bus, train or other commuting options for your children.

Advise your children to avoid obvious displays of wealth publicly and to travel with friends if possible until they know and understand the surroundings. One of our expat families living in Beijing recently recounted the story of their child's bicycle being stolen that was left outside the front of their apartment complex, despite the fact that the bike was chained up.

Equally important is explaining to your children the following:

- Although they are in unfamiliar territory, they should not talk to strangers.

- At home, keep an easily accessible list for your kids of where they can find important phone numbers, friends in Expatland, their teacher, police and so on. Also advise them what to do in the event of fire, sickness or an intruder if they find themselves in a situation where they need to take action themselves.

- They should learn basic foreign language expressions as they may need to get out of difficult situations and/or call for assistance or seek directions.

Personal & Family Protection

Depending where you live in Expatland, your security risks need careful consideration. If the risk is serious, you may decide you need personal protection.

Apart from self-defence classes, you and your family may need 24-hour security protection. When selecting security personnel, speak to trusted sources and if security is not provided through your company, then you should ask other expats using such a service. Local law enforcement officers could also be helpful in the selection process.

From a legal perspective, keep in mind that you need to review the ramifications of using and working with personal security guards in Expatland. This can be done by obtaining legal advice from a suitably qualified solicitor, by speaking with your employer and/or with local police officers.

AT A GLANCE

- It is important to be aware of security risks in Expatland and take appropriate security measures.
- In some countries, normally innocuous activities take on a much higher degree of risk, such as a single woman walking through a market.
- Have a well-prepared plan of action in case you need it.
- Have a readily accessible list of major points of contact, such as fire, police and emergency services.
- Keep duplicate copies of key documents in a safe but accessible place for the family.
- Make sure that your home country advisors and family members know how to access your important information online or elsewhere as needed.
- Educate yourself on the political and security situation in your part of Expatland, preferably before you arrive.
- At airport terminals, be cautious about strangers who are overly friendly.
- Always be aware of your surroundings. After a long flight there is a temptation to relax upon landing. This can be the time when you can be taken advantage of.
- If you are driving in a new country, always get a GPS and/or if possible make sure you have someone to meet you.
- When travelling in Expatland or on holidays, never leave your kids alone or with people you are not very well acquainted with.

- Only use home staff from a reputable service. Make sure they have permission to be working in Expatland. Keep an easily accessible file containing a copy of their passport and other details just in case you need to refer to them.
- Learn about the area you are going to live in and its history, including the ethnic makeup of the inhabitants. Find out as much as you can about the physical environment such as proximity to police, the fire brigade, hospital and ambulance.
- Acquaint yourself with bus, train or other commuting options for your children to and from school.
- Advise your children to avoid obvious displays of wealth publicly when outside the home.
- Remind them that they should not talk to strangers, even though they are in an unfamiliar environment.
- At home, keep an easily accessible list for your kids of where they can find important phone numbers, friends in Expatland, their teacher, police and so on. Also advise them what to do in the event of fire, sickness or an intruder.
- If security is an issue, you may decide you need personal protection. When selecting security personnel, vet them carefully.
- Check into the legal ramifications of using personal security guards.

12

EXPATLAND STRUCTURES

'Expatland structures' is the term I have given to the potential use of a company, trust or a pension fund that may be established to hold investment assets. Once you have arrived in Expatland and understood any legal and business risks, it is important to consider what structure, if any, you should establish for accumulated assets to protect your wealth.

CST Tax Advisors has assisted expats with tax and financial management strategies involving structures for a number of years. Most of the time, expats – particularly those who move around from location to Expatland location – will wish to acquire assets in a variety of jurisdictions. This usually leads to a discussion about how to acquire such assets. Hence family trusts, companies or foundations are often part of the solution.

Consider the example of an expat who may be a director of his family company in Singapore. That directorship usually brings with it potential liability for debts of the company under a given range of circumstances. If such an expat fails to structure himself correctly, an adverse court judgement could see personal assets in the firing line.

Case Study

Recently we had an expat client approach us for assistance as they were in an unenviable position with respect to a trading company and wanted advice.

The expat client was the only director of a Singapore company. In Singapore, if you are appointed as a local director – and you are the only local director as was the case with this client – you are unable to resign.

Hence the expat client was being pursued by a landlord of a commercial building for rent that the company had failed to pay that amounted to more than SGD$250,000.

In this case, while the expat client had other 'friends' of his that were shareholders – they were neither directors nor resident in Singapore. Thus it was the expat client in Singapore who was exposed for the trading liabilities of the company.

In circumstances such as the above, holding personal assets in his name meant that the landlord to the company was ultimately able to access those assets following a judgement being issued in their favour.

This example highlights the need for asset protection structures.

Exposure to personal risk can also result from holding assets directly. For example, in some states in the US it exposes the landowner to liability for any damage done to neighbouring property or damage done on the property. Holding property in the US in your own name, rather than the name of a trust or corporation, does not make commercial sense if there are risks attached to assets ownership.

Part of the journey to Expatland is to look at how you should own assets and what potential structures those assets should be held in. When it comes to holding assets, the following is a description of some commonly used structures:

A Discretionary Trust

Often referred to as a family trust, a discretionary trust is the most popular structure when used for family wealth management.

A discretionary trust allows the trustee to exercise discretion on an annual basis as to which beneficiaries will receive a distribution and to what extent each beneficiary shall benefit. This can be very useful as it gives the family a wide degree of flexibility about who receives income.

A Unit Trust

A unit trust provides that beneficiaries have fixed entitlements as set out under the deed of trust.

Unit trusts are commonly used when arm's length parties wish to enter into a commercial undertaking together.

Each party's entitlement to income and capital from the trust is proportionate to the units held.

A Hybrid Trust

A hybrid trust is a combination between a unit trust and a discretionary trust. It contains elements of fixed entitlements and/or rights and discretionary elements. For example, there may be units that are issued to a unit holder that gives them an entitlement to income but not to capital gains.

There may be units that provide direct voting rights, but no rights to income and/or capital. Hence hybrid trusts are very flexible structures.

A Superannuation/Pension Fund

A superannuation fund or pension fund is a form of trust usually formed under common law in which individuals accumulate income for retirement.

They are very effective structures for long-term planning. In many countries these types of structures are able to access tax concessions.

A Company

A company is a type of entity that has a distinct legal existence from its owners. The owners of the company are known as shareholders. Its legal status gives a company the same rights as a natural person, which means that a company can incur debts, and both sue and be sued.

Companies are managed by company officers who are called directors and company secretaries.

Generally speaking, individuals and global expats use a type of company structure called a private limited company. This type of company does not sell its shares to the public and has limited liability.

A Foundation

In general, most foundations are companies limited by guarantee or trusts. They can be formed in civil law jurisdictions or common law jurisdictions. Usually foundations are charitable undertakings.

In the case of foundations that are trusts, as trusts have no legal personality it is the trustee of the foundation that acts on behalf of the foundation. In many countries foundations are not required to register with any public authority. Unlike civil law systems the term has no precise meaning in common law jurisdictions.

A Partnership

A partnership is an association of people who carry on an investment or business activity as partners. In some countries merely receiving income jointly can qualify you as being in a partnership for tax purposes. A partnership is relatively easy and inexpensive to establish and operate. A formal partnership agreement is common, but not essential. One of the features of a partnership if it is a 'general partnership' is personal liability for debts of the partnership. In most cases this means that a partner is responsible for the debts of the partnership, even if they did not directly incur or cause the debt. This is to be contrasted with a 'limited partnership' in which you can have limited partners and general partners. In limited partnerships liability is limited to the amount of capital contributed to the partnership.

These structures commonly used in Expatland are generally always part of a planning exercise.

For my clients, I advise them that their balance sheet should be viewed from the perspective of pre-arrival and post-arrival. Consideration needs to be given to the laws of Expatland where the client is going to reside and whether or not some assets might be transferred or 'settled' into any of the above structures. This could be appropriate if there were asset protection or tax planning reasons for doing so.

Having deemed what type of structures could be used theoretically, the next issue of consideration for the expat is what jurisdictions the particular structures should be established in. Some of the top commonly used jurisdictions include Hong Kong, Singapore, Cyprus, Cook Islands, Cayman Islands, Mauritius, Jersey, Luxembourg and Delaware.

While these jurisdictions all have different legal and tax regimes, they have a number of common features including:

- Favourable asset protection laws
- Minimal disclosure obligations, which can assist in ensuring privacy in respect of your personal assets
- Good legal regimes based on common law
- Recognised areas of expertise.

The following are some comments on each of these regimes:

Hong Kong

Hong Kong is sometimes erroneously thought of as an offshore jurisdiction. It does have a number of features that may provide this impression, but for the most part it is a vibrant, strong, business focused economy that offers many competitive advantages.

It does have an attractive legal and tax regime. Income is taxed under the 'territorial principle'. This means that only income arising in or derived from Hong Kong is taxable in the jurisdiction.

Hong Kong therefore is a popular location for formation of investment entities and trusts and holding companies.

Further benefits to the jurisdiction are its minimal company law disclosure obligations with respect to beneficial owners, tax-free status for capital gains and non-taxation of offshore income.

Many global expats use the Hong Kong banking system to protect family wealth, as there is an abundance of private and retail banks in the territory.

Hong Kong also has a number of advantages unrelated to law and taxation. Its proximity to China is a key advantage and many international businesses use Hong Kong for strategic market access in North and South East Asia.

Until recently a Hong Kong company could use only a corporate director. While that requirement has now changed and at least one individual director is required to be a director of the Hong Kong company, this person need not reside in Hong Kong. This is unlike other countries, including Singapore and Australia, where the individual needs to reside in the jurisdiction.

The increasing pace with which China is allowing its markets to open up is a positive long-term factor for the Hong Kong economy. Major infrastructure is continuing to be developed to facilitate the movement of people by land between Hong Kong, Shanghai, Beijing and other cities in China.

Singapore

Singapore has become a major financial and business centre in Asia Pacific over the past 25 years. It is also a global hub for shipping, IT and logistic services. It has a common law regime and its arbitration and court system is highly regarded.

Similar to Hong Kong it has favourable tax rules, the absence of a capital gains tax and no tax on interest income for individuals.

Infrastructure, telecommunications and transport are excellent. For smaller investment companies generally an audit is not required where shareholders are natural persons. Singapore does, however, require a local director for its private companies. In 2004 Singapore established a licensed trust regime that has since developed. However, unlike some more long-standing jurisdictions, Singapore trusts do not have specific statutory provisions with respect to foreign judgements and other features as will be discussed in the following section.

In terms of Exchange of Information, Singapore has begun a phase of making information more readily available to foreign governments and revenue authorities. Its private banking industry is very well developed and all of the top 20 global private banks have offices in Singapore.

Both individuals and companies are able to access a wide variety of tax incentives on offer from various government departments.

Cyprus

While Cyprus remains a popular jurisdiction for professional services, trust services, tourism and leisure, the country has developed a promising gas industry.

The country is part of the European Union (EU) and it is a sound, independent democratic republic and a member of the Commonwealth.

The Cyprus Government is committed to creating a competitive and favourable offshore tax regime while at the same time maintaining a comprehensive domestic economy.

Cyprus has double tax agreements with more than 40 other countries, including most major Western countries and most Central and Eastern European states.

One of the consequences of a broad treaty network is that Cyprus has developed a sound Holding Company Regime for Global business. English is widely spoken and the legal system of Cyprus is based on English common law.

Cook Islands

The Cook Islands are located in the South Pacific Ocean due south of Hawaii. Named after Captain James Cook, the English explorer, the country consists of 15 islands spread over 1m square miles of ocean.

The island of Rarotonga is the capital, and home to more than 60 per cent of the population. English is the everyday language.

Originally a colony of Britain, then New Zealand, the Cook Islands achieved limited self-government in 1957, and became 'self-governing in free association' with New Zealand in 1965. It is now a fully sovereign state with its own parliament, universal suffrage, and general elections every four years. All Cook Islanders hold dual New Zealand and Cook Islands nationality and the country continues to enjoy a close relationship with New Zealand.

The judicial system in the Cook Islands is highly regarded. The Court system is hierarchical, beginning with the High Court, the Court of Appeal, and a further and final right of appeal to the Privy Council in England. All judges are senior judges chosen from the Court of Appeal in New Zealand.

The offshore centre was established in 1981 initially targeting markets in Australasia and driven by merchant banking transactions. In 1989 the Cook Islands became the first country to introduce asset protection laws and it remains the leading jurisdiction for asset protection trusts. This industry now dominates the financial centre.

The Cook Islands are in the same time zone as Hawaii, making it particularly well placed for doing business with US-based clients. While the Cook Islands are geographically isolated, they have excellent connections with the rest of the world with modern communication systems and regular flights to Los Angeles, Tahiti and Auckland.

The thriving offshore industry is a major contributor to total government revenue. The other important contributors to the economy are tourism and cultured pearl farming.

Cayman Islands

Similar to other Caribbean islands, the Cayman Islands are an English-speaking Dependent Territory of the UK. They are situated in the Caribbean between Cuba and Central America and are politically stable.

The Cayman Islands has one of largest banking centres in the world. Indeed, its trust industry manages significant global capital.

For the private client, the Cayman Islands offer many advantages including English law and a good reputation for consistent bureaucratic treatment.

There are no exchange controls and many international trusts and companies are formed in the jurisdiction to hold global assets.

One of the growth industries in recent times has been the hedge fund industry. Many investment and managed funds that are held by global expats in Expatland are managed here.

The Cayman Islands has recently begun entering Taxation Information Exchange Agreements like other offshore tax centres.

Mauritius

Mauritius is located in the Indian Ocean and has a population of approximately 1.2m.

It was a colony of both France and Britain and as a result the population is fluent in English and French. As with other former English colonies the Republic of Mauritius operates as a democracy, similar to the Westminster system.

Unusually Mauritius is one of the few countries popular with global expats that operates a hybrid legal system based on English and French law.

The law relating to criminal and civil litigation procedures is mainly English, while the main bodies of substantial law are based on the civil law of the French Napoleonic code. Company law is based on the common law of England and New Zealand. Mauritius also has a wide range of double tax agreements.

This ensures that it is a popular choice for holding companies and those companies seeking to access a number of proximate countries including India and Africa. Investing in India in particular has a number of advantages when using Mauritius as the jurisdiction to transact from.

There are a wide variety of company types and the operation of the accounting, legal and financial regimes are certain in their operation.

Jersey

Jersey has for many years played a role in protecting private wealth and being used as a trust and company regime.

It has attracted high net worth individuals because it offers not only proximity to the UK and Europe, but tax incentives and a stable business and living environment.

There is no company tax in Jersey for most activities; however, certain financial business activities do have a tax rate of 10 per cent on their profits. A clear advantage working in Jersey's favour is that it is not the EU.

Like other jurisdictions, Jersey has over recent years entered in Taxation Information Exchange Agreements as part of its efforts to combat terrorism, tax evasion and money laundering schemes.

However, for the global expat Jersey offers a strong banking system, a highly sophisticated legal regime and easy travel options.

Luxembourg

In 1815 Luxembourg was created within the German Bund by the treaty of Vienna. Luxembourg gained its independence from Germany in 1867 and became a constitutional monarchy with the legislative power vested in a democratically elected parliament. (Its capital city is also called Luxembourg.)

Luxembourg is a member of the European Union and the OECD.

Its strategic geographic location in the heart of Europe, political stability, its multicultural and highly qualified workforce together with a strong legal environment and attractive tax framework have been key factors for establishing Luxembourg as a hub for international trade in the financial sector and in industrial and commercial activities.

The law operates under the model of the Napoleonic code and it provides similar outcomes to the Belgian and French legal systems.

Evidence of Luxembourg's progressive policy approach can be seen through its ability to adapt to change. An example of this is the creation of a new family estate management vehicle created in 2007.

This vehicle was designated as Société de Gestion de Patrimoine Familial (SPF). It is aimed at the management of the estates of private individuals.

Luxembourg has also implemented numerous domestic legal rules to help investors and businesses alike. These rules facilitate Luxembourg positioning itself as a primary place in Europe to establish companies pursuing a holding activity, the commonly called Sociétés de Participation Financières (SOPARFI).

Delaware

When considering where to establish a tax-effective vehicle many people use Delaware, in the US.

Delaware provides a number of advantages including flexible business law and no state corporate income tax if you do not do business in Delaware. There is no personal income tax for non-residents of Delaware. Neither shareholders or company officers or managers need to live in Delaware to establish a Delaware corporation.

Delaware has a unique court system in that it does not use juries. Rather judges decide court cases. The Court of Chancery only hears business cases.

Companies formed in Delaware also have the benefit of not being subject to sales tax or property tax.

The Delaware company would be popular for US-based residents of Expatland seeking to invest in the US or elsewhere.

There are more Delaware companies than in any other state. The cost of incorporation is relatively inexpensive.

It is not the purpose of this book to present a more detailed analysis of these countries but rather to say that when considering which part of Expatland you might establish you personal structures in, any competent advisor working with you should conduct a review of at least three regimes on your behalf.

They will then be in a position to present the pros and cons of setting up in that regime. They will also be able to advise why structuring of your assets in a certain way can assist you moving forward, not only with financial issues while you are alive but also the management of your estate when you are gone.

As unpleasant as that prospect is, having your assets held in a safe, secure reliable structure that can be managed by trusted advisors and family members is sometimes a very desirable outcome for an expat, especially if there has been a second marriage, with young children remaining. Asset protection structures can also protect your assets after death if there is a challenge to some inheritance or similar family property dispute.

Expat structures are a very important consideration as part of the journey to Expatland.

AT A GLANCE

- Once you have arrived in Expatland and have understood the legal and business risks that may occur, it is important to consider what structure, if any, you should establish to accumulate assets to protect your wealth.
- If an expat fails to structure correctly, an adverse judgement could see personal assets being put at risk.
- These structures, such as a hybrid trust or a discretionary trust, are commonly used in Expatland and will always be part of the planning exercise.
- Your balance sheet should be viewed from the perspective of pre-arrival to Expatland and post-arrival.
- Consideration needs to be given to the particular law of your Expatland and whether or not some assets should be put into any of the structures.
- After deciding on structures, the next issue for the expat is what jurisdictions the particular structures should be established in.
- Any competent advisor – tax, legal or accounting – should conduct a review of at least three jurisdictions in order to provide you with the best advice.
- Having the appropriate structure for your assets will protect them after your death from family disputes or otherwise.

13

EXPATLAND TAXATION

There are many important strategic considerations when analysing and managing the tax implications of moving country or changing residency status.

The following are key concepts* when it comes to expat taxation:

- Income
- Capital
- Territorial taxation
- Global taxation
- Controlled foreign corporations
- International trust
- Passive income
- Active income.

* Each of these terms is defined in Appendix A, 'Special Terms'.

It is important to understand and plan for the tax systems of your home country and Expatland. Specifically, there are six considerations that should always be addressed:

1. Does your home country tax you when you exit your home jurisdiction and change tax residency?

2. Does your home country levy tax on your income when you are living overseas and, if so, what are the consequences of this?

3. If you are not taxed on your foreign income and foreign assets by your home country, how will the income and assets you hold be taxed in the arrival country? For example, you may have a share portfolio in your home country that is not taxed in your arrival country.

4. If your home country assets – such as real estate or shares – rise in value and are sold while you are a resident in Expatland, what are the tax consequences?

5. If you own assets in a third country (meaning a country that is not your home country or your arrival country), what are the tax implications for you selling those assets in that third country?

These are just some of the many questions you need to consider when moving from your home country to a different country. Failure to plan and understand the impact of these questions could add thousands of dollars to your global tax bill. Unfortunately, this cost may not be evident until years after a move to Expatland.

One recent case of mine involved a client moving from Singapore to the US. The expatriate had real estate in a third country, namely Australia, and that real estate was acquired many years earlier for a much lower cost.

When the expatriate moved to the US, the property had increased significantly in value and the client decided to sell the property, as they wanted to access the capital that had accrued.

In this case although the client had only recently arrived in their Expatland, the sale of the property would have resulted in a large capital gains tax exposure in the US.

Fortunately, we were able to save the client from committing a serious mistake due to their lack of understanding of US tax law.

In many respects this is unjust, as most of the 'capital appreciation' occurred at a time when the client was not even a resident of the US. The capital gains tax would have eroded much of the value the client wanted to access.

In another case a client was in receipt of pension income from their home country. Such income was not taxed in their home country and as a result the client was able to live comfortably. Unfortunately, when the client moved to Expatland the whole amount of the pension was taxable and as they had not considered this issue before their move to Expatland – their lifestyle was severely affected due to the tax burden in Expatland.

Developing a tax strategy around arriving in Expatland and departing from your home country is very important and cannot be overemphasised.

Taxation planning is essential when your home country has an exit tax regime. Generally speaking, an 'exit tax regime' is a regime that deems you as having sold your assets merely by changing tax residency. This can mean that your capital gains on assets you hold will be crystallised when you cease being a resident in a particular country. Now different countries have different rules about ceasing tax residency, so it is important that you examine this point from the perspective of your home country.

Sometimes these exit tax regimes may treat you as not having a liability to pay tax on these assets until you dispose of them, which may be many years after you have left your home country.

As an example, let's take a look at expatriate couple Mr & Mrs Jones who plan a five-year move for work purposes. They have a share portfolio of $500,000 and they move from their home country to Expatland. At the time of their departure, there is an unrealised capital gain within the share portfolio of $50,000. (Note that for the purpose of this example, there is a capital gains regime in their home country.)

At the time of leaving their home country, they were unaware that the 'exit tax regime' applied to treat their shares as being taxable in their home country at the time of their departure – if they chose to include an amount in their income tax return for the year of their departure. Hence for the year in which they moved to Expatland, the couple did not include any amount of capital gain in their personal income tax returns.

Now five years later the value of the Jones' share portfolio is now $1 million and the amount of the unrealised capital gain is $550,000. They now want to sell the share portfolio to buy a property in their arrival country.

If they do so, under the rules of their home country they will have to pay capital gains tax on the full amount of the unrealised profit. This result came as a shock to Mr & Mrs Jones, who thought they had left their tax exposures to their former home country behind! This is a common event and one example of failing to plan.

In this scenario the couple, practically speaking, have a few options available to them to consider.

One option may be that instead of selling their share portfolio and triggering a capital gain, they may be able to use the shares as security and indeed borrow against the shares to use the equity that has built up in the shares. Another option might be that they may be able to amend their income tax returns in the year of their departure and seek to pay a much lower amount of capital gains tax.

This, of course, has to be considered from the perspective of the tax laws applicable in Expatland; however, these may be possible solutions.

Arriving in Expatland

Following your departure from your home country, it is essential that you consider the tax consequences of arriving in Expatland. This is particularly the case if you have assets in multiple jurisdictions.

You need to consider how those assets might need to be rearranged before tax residency commences in the new jurisdiction. For example, an expat moving to Expatland may be able to establish complying foreign companies and/or trusts that keep international assets out of the tax jurisdiction applicable to Expatland.

Some Expatland jurisdictions only subject income to tax if it is remitted or deemed to be remitted to the jurisdiction. Hence establishing a properly structured foreign company or trust may eliminate any form of tax exposure in Expatland.

Many people take the view – in the case of expatriate clients – that it is morally fair that they can choose to protect the value of their assets they acquired before moving to Expatland and where possible lower their personal cost within the law if there is an opportunity to do so.

This is particularly the case if the expat intends to remain in Expatland for only a few years before returning to their home country. In my view, an expatriate client should not pay more tax than is considered necessary just for the privilege of living in Expatland.

An expatriate unwittingly paying more tax merely by living or working overseas for four or five years can, in fact, reduce a lot of the economic incentive of uprooting their lives and moving from their home country.

Many global expatriates struggle to find a tax firm that can provide home country taxation support as well as continuing their services in Expatland. (CST Tax Advisors can assist you in both your home country and Expatland.)

Unfortunately, we see on a regular basis the adverse consequences of expatriates unwittingly caught up in the interaction of global tax systems.

Some countries operate their tax system on a schedular system whereby tax rates for certain types of income are higher than tax rates of others. For example, the tax rate applicable to capital gains or interest income may be lower than the tax on employment income.

Other countries offer the opportunity for contracts to be structured on the basis that work done in the country is taxed, whereas work done outside the country is not taxable.

It is clearly the case that in tax systems such as these, thought and attention should be given to how employment income is to be taxed and particular care given to how share options, either vested or unvested shares, will be taxed in the arrival country.

Many large corporations provide executive stock options or access to employee share programs. Careful planning needs to be undertaken to understand your tax position.

The Big 4

While many residents of Expatland have their personal income tax returns prepared by the Big 4 Firms under global tax programs, often this is not a satisfying experience for a number of reasons. These are:

1. The Big 4 Firm is usually retained by the employer organisation, not the expat executive. Hence the exercise is about minimising risk from the perspective of the employer rather than thinking about things from the perspective of the employee.

2. The person who usually prepares the income tax return often works from a set template. It is our experience that they do not consider how to optimise the home country

exit tax issues for the expat or how to assist the expat plan their arrival in Expatland. Often the expat is expected to essentially complete the income tax return by filling out copious schedules of information.

3. During the period of time that the expat is in Expatland, it is not often the case that the employee of the Big 4 Firm will work with your tax advisor in your home country to integrate your tax issues on an annual basis. (By the use of the term 'integrate', I mean the process of annual collaboration and co-operation between the tax advisor in your home country and the tax advisor in Expatland.)

This lack of integration in the manner in which tax advisory and compliance services are delivered often leaves expats exposed when it comes to identifying tax issues and planning opportunities. One example that we saw recently occurred when a client of ours wanted to sell an asset in their home country. They approached us to work with the foreign Big 4 firm to see what could be done to lessen the tax bill in the foreign jurisdiction. Our personnel were not able to deal directly with the foreign office of the Big 4 firm. It was outside the scope of work of this Big 4 firm. Hence our client and ourselves had to spend considerable time with another accounting firm in Expatland to consider and understand their options for the sale of the asset and work out how and when to do it and over what time period. In the final event we were able to work out a good solution for the client.

This lack of 'integration' between the Big 4 and home country advisors can cause practical issues that result in more tax being paid than necessary. In this case, it was to the client's advantage not to use the Big 4 firm, although their employer was covering its fees, and work with the foreign firm we identified and pay the costs personally.

Given the manner in which global employers often retain the Big 4 accounting firms, these companies cannot operate on the basis of providing integrated personal tax services to executives in these global tax preparation programs. Many issues exist outside the mere preparation of the Expatland personal tax return.

Timing of Residency

Some jurisdictions treat a foreign company as being a resident of the arrival country if the majority of directors reside in that country. For example, Mr & Mrs Brown, residents of country A, move to Expatland B.

Expatland tax laws operate so that a foreign company is resident where 'central management and control' is exercised. As the couple now reside in Expatland, they exercise 'central management and control' from Expatland. Hence the company is a resident of Expatland and income of the foreign company is now taxable in Expatland.

That foreign company now has tax, accounting and filing obligations simply because the directors of the company moved to Expatland.

This is a case where a pre-migration tax planning opportunity exists. It might be wise to restructure the board of the company so that income is not taxable in Expatland.

Taxation in Expatland is complex. With Expatland's population of more than 230 million people, there are a multitude of tax and legal systems to consider.

Allow Time to Plan

Anyone considering a move to Expatland should try to allow at least six months before implementing the move. This is because there is an enormous amount of tax planning to be done, including the development of the tax plan and the preparation of checklists to answer any questions raised prior to entry, which are all a key part of getting taxation in Expatland right. Even if you are going to a tax-free jurisdiction, thought and planning is still required and you need to allow sufficient time for this.

Expatland Trusts

Trusts are a useful planning vehicle when it comes to holding assets on a global basis. Some information on trusts is set out here. However, it is not an exhaustive explanation of the legal and taxation issues associated with trusts, but it is a useful introduction if you are considering establishing a trust. It is important that you obtain further advice from a legal practitioner.

In essence a trust is simply a relationship where one person (the trustee) is under an obligation and holds assets (trust property) for the benefit of another person (a beneficiary) for some object or purpose. A trust has four essential elements:

1. Trustee
2. Trust Property
3. Equitable Obligation
4. Beneficiaries.

To re-state these elements in slightly more legalistic terms "a trust is a fiduciary relationship where one person, a trustee, holds an interest in property but has an equitable obligation to use or keep that property for the benefit of another person(s) (beneficiaries) for some committed object or purpose.

Types of Trusts

There are many types of trusts; however, the common ones are:

- Express Trusts
- Settled Trust
- Discretionary Trusts
- Unit Trust
- Will Trust.

Express Trusts: These are trusts created by the express and intentional declaration of the settlor. Trusts dealt with in practice usually evidence this declaration by way of a formal trust deed.

Settled Trust: One form of an express trust is a settled trust created by settlor (or director). The settlor will intentionally create a trust by gifting the initial trust property to be held on trust by a trustee under an equitable obligation.

The most common trusts CST Tax Advisors implement are discretionary trusts, unit trusts and Will trusts (or deceased estates).

Discretionary Trust: A common settled trust dealt with in practice is a discretionary trust. A discretionary trust, which may also be known as a family trust, allows the trustee (who is usually the head of the family) to exercise discretion on an annual basis as to which beneficiaries will receive a distribution and to what extent each beneficiary shall benefit.

Unit Trust: Unit trusts are commonly used when arm's length parties wish to enter into a commercial undertaking together. Each party's entitlement to income and capital from the trust is proportionate to the units held.

Will Trust: A Will trust or a deceased estate arises on the death of a person. Upon death, property of the deceased passes to their estate. The fiduciary obligation to administer the estate and the assets therefore falls upon the executor or administrator who assumes the role of trustee in respect of the property of the deceased estate.

The beneficiaries of a deceased are those nominated in the Will of the deceased.

Why Choose a Trust?

When you are choosing a trust, the following are some issues you need to consider:

- Control
- Simplicity/complexity
- Liability limitation

- Costs – establishment and maintenance
- Life span
- Formalities/adherence to rules
- Reporting and disclosure requirements
- Acceptability to financiers
- Admission of new investors
- Selling out/winding up
- Family disharmony/asset – sheltering
- Retirement planning
- Ease of future restructure.

Trust Taxation Issues

If the concept of a trust satisfies your commercial objectives, you would need to consider the following taxation issues:

- Overall level of tax
- Acceptability by authorities
- Double taxation
- Restructuring tax consequences

- Employee on costs
- Tax payments/tax rate
- Flexibility of distributions
- Tax losses trapped
- Dividend streaming
- Type of business to be carried on.

How to Set Up a Trust

If you have made the decision that a trust is an appropriate structure for your needs, the next step is to establish a trust by using a competent professional. Before approaching such a professional you should not only have considered the commercial and taxation issues noted previously, but you should also have determined the purpose and activities of the trust; the nominated beneficiaries and future beneficiaries; and who is to be the trustee and settlor.

The professional (trust company or solicitor) will draft the trust deed in accordance with your requirements and at this stage it is critical that a thorough review is done to ensure that the trust deed (or governing rules) reflects your commercial and legal requirements and allows flexibility for future contingencies.

At this stage it is critical that you read through the draft deed and that questions are addressed prior to creating the trust. In this regard, your family or business solicitor may be used to add their comments and to provide a different perspective and extra level of comfort to you.

Parties to a Trust

The following is an explanation of the different parties to a trust:

The Settlor: The settlor is the person who brings the trust into being. Typically the settlor is a family friend or business associate who will contribute initial capital to settle the trust. In some countries it is important that there is not any reimbursement by the trustee in respect of distributions made for children under 18 years old if a parent, who will usually act as trustee or a director of the trustee company of a family trust, settles or creates the trust.

It is also advisable that the advisors to the trust are not the settlor, for the reason that many trust deeds contain clauses that the settlor is excluded from any benefit or income under the trust.

The Trustee: A trustee is the person who holds an interest in trust property for a committed trust object or purpose. In a discretionary trust situation the trustee exercises control over trust property so the trustee can deal with it on behalf of beneficiaries.

The choice of a trustee is worth proper consideration for the reason that the trustee's powers and duties are significant. In that regard, the person who is appointed to the position must understand their role and responsibilities. Trustees may be individuals, but more commonly will be companies to limit liability. In a family trust, a parent or both parents will usually act as directors of a corporate trustee.

The Appointor or Protector: The appointor or protector is the person or persons who have the authority under the trust deed to appoint or remove the trustee of the trust. As such, the appointor is often said to be the controller of the trust. Many trust deeds empower the appointor to remove the trustee and appoint a new trustee at any time in writing.

Unless specified in the trust deed or in the will of the appointor, on the death of the appointor, the legal personal representative of the deceased appointor will become the appointor.

Income Beneficiaries: These are beneficiaries who may at the discretion of the trustee receive entitlement to trust income. Most modern trust deeds are drafted very broadly in this area to give the trustee very wide discretionary powers for the advantage of flexibility of distribution for taxation purposes. Common classes of beneficiaries are:

- Family members, including children
- Unborn children of family members, such as direct lineal descendants
- Eligible entities in which the above-mentioned beneficiaries of the trust itself has an interest (such as a corporate beneficiary).

Capital Beneficiaries: These are beneficiaries who are entitled to the corpus of the trust or the capital in the trust. This entitlement does not usually arise until vesting day, or the day the trust is to be wound up, but entitlements to capital or corpus of the trust may occur earlier if permitted by the trust deed or agreed to by all beneficiaries.

Default Beneficiaries: A default beneficiary is simply the beneficiary to whom a distribution may default to in the absence of any other nominated beneficiary.

For example, should an amended assessment be raised increasing assessable income, that income will be distributed primarily in accordance with the relevant trustee's distribution statement. However, in the absence of any guidance contained therein or in the event the resolution cannot be located or was not made for the reason there was considered to be no income, the distribution may revert to the default beneficiary rather than be assessed in the hands of the trustee at the top marginal rate.

There are very few restrictions on who may be a beneficiary. A beneficiary may be a resident or non-resident natural person (such as a company) or any legal entity. Further, persons who have not yet been born or legal entities that have not yet come into existence may subsequently become beneficiaries. However, it is important to nominate who will be and who can become a beneficiary on drafting of the deed.

A trust, as stated earlier, is a fiduciary relationship. The adding of unanticipated beneficiaries at a later stage may, in a worst case scenario, lead to a resettlement of a trust or the ceasing of the former relationship and creation of a new relationship, being the creation of a new trust. Should there be considered to be cessation of one trust and the creation of a new trust, a myriad of unwelcome income tax, capital tax and stamp duty issues may arise. Thus, upon reviewing the deed detailed consideration must be given to who might potentially become income, capital and/or default beneficiaries.

Income Tax & Other Tax Compliance & Planning

Our view is always that tax should never be the 'be all and end all'.

At CST Tax Advisors, wherever possible we try to avoid a tax decision driving a financial decision.

As an example, in some countries the rate on long-term capital gains is lower than the tax rate applicable to assets bought and sold with one year.

This then can provide some sort of incentive for clients to hold onto an asset – for example, shares – longer so they can access a lower tax rate.

Consider the case where the long-term capital gain tax rate for a country is say 20 per cent whereas the short-term capital gains tax rate is 35 per cent. If an expat client has a share portfolio with a capital gain in it of US$200,000 – they may be tempted to hold out until they have held the shares for more than one year, for instance. That is, they have the intention to sell the shares but not wanting to pay a 35 per cent rate of tax causes them to hold the charges for a longer period of time. The problem with this approach can be that holding the shares for, say, six months more ignores what is actually happening in the stock market.

Often clients see adverse movements in the share price – while waiting for a lower tax rate! Hence we often see tax decisions driving financial decisions. In this case, the right time to sell may be when the tax rate is 15 per cent higher – as the price of the shares may actually fall by more than the tax difference.

So it is worth remembering that tax is one element of a decision, not the whole decision.

That said, the effect of tax leakage on your family income can be significant, and it is important to understand how much tax you will pay on a global basis and to consider if any steps can be taken to minimise the tax cost in a legal and complying manner.

One strategy that can be useful, particularly if you are moving to a low tax country, is to pay the tax saving into a separate bank account and/or reduce existing loans. Acting as if you are paying the same amount of tax as you do in your home country is often a good way of not spending the difference!

Many overseas jurisdictions have other taxes, such as property tax, wealth tax and estate tax, so make sure you understand all the taxes that can apply in your part of Expatland.

While lower rates of income tax often can be a motivating force to move to Expatland, be wary and recognise that other taxes can reduce your wealth apart from income tax. In Denmark, for example, a client with a large property portfolio in his home country was shocked to discover that this 'pre-migration asset base' was exposed to death taxes in Denmark.

In cases such as this, one strategy that may be worth discussing with your private banker or wealth advisor is to take out additional life insurance to cover any such sudden tax exposures.

Zero Tax Regimes

For those expats moving to a part of Expatland where there are no taxes, you should be aware that there might still be some tax exposure in your home country. An example of popular zero tax regimes include the United Arab Emirates, Monaco and exotic islands in the Caribbean.

Some years ago we had a client come to our firm with a tax issue that needed addressing. In this case the client had worked in one of the Gulf States for more than two years. He erroneously believed that such income would be exempt from tax in his home country.

Unfortunately, the lack of tax in the Gulf State resulted in the income remaining taxable in his home country. Specifically, he had failed to properly exit his home jurisdiction:

- He had not given up his former home.
- He retained his car in his former home country.
- He remained on the electoral role.
- He had kept a number of home country club memberships.
- He visited his home country on more than eight occasions and had stayed in his family home.
- He was living in serviced accommodation in Expatland and kept all his financial assets in his home country.

When the taxation authority issued tax assessments to him, he then came to us seeking advice. These tax assessments unfortunately had eroded a lot of the benefit of his moving away from friends and family to earn the higher tax-free income in Expatland.

US Citizens

As a special note for US tax persons or for those holding a Green Card but living outside the US, you will remain taxable regardless of leaving your home country.

While there may be concessions for, say, a 'homestead allowance' or other benefits, Green Card holders and persons of the US need to be aware that out of sight is not out of mind as far as the IRS is concerned.

One of the recent developments in the US tax system has been the imposition of an 'exit tax' for those Green Card holders who give up their Green Card and have held it for more than eight years.

It is not the function of this book to provide US taxation advice; however, we draw to your attention that ceasing US residency by way of returning your Green Card can have the effect of triggering US exit taxes.

Double Tax Agreements

Double tax agreements (DTAs) generally exist to prevent fiscal evasion and double taxation. These agreements either follow the OECD model or the US model agreement.

Often the main function of the DTA is to decide how someone who may be viewed as a resident of both countries should be categorised for the purpose of income tax in one or the other country.

Tax Treaty Residency Issues

When deciding how a DTA applies, you do need to identify your tax residency. This is usually Article 4 under most treaties.

By way of background, most DTAs will have provisions that deal with pensions, annuities, government payments or social security payments. It is also important to remember that each DTA is unique. Simply because one DTA allows a certain treatment does not mean another will allow the same treatment.

Your residency determines how treaty articles on pensions and annuities will be applied. Generally the first step is to apply the domestic laws of each country to identify your residency.

If, after applying the domestic law of each country, you are a resident of both countries, apply the tiebreaker rules (see Appendix A, 'Special Terms', for the meaning of 'tiebreaker rules'). These include:

- In which country do you have a permanent home available to you?
- With which country do you have closer personal and economic relations?
- In which country do you have a habitual abode?
- Of which country are you a national?

If none of these tiebreaker rules work, then residency will be decided by the competent authorities of each country upon request by the taxpayer.

Some treaties have special rules – for example, the US/Canada and the US/UK treaties have special rules for taxpayers who have US Green Cards.

If you are a US citizen, you also may need to refer to the so-called 'saving clause' (typically found in Article 1) for special rules that allow the US to tax in some cases as if the treaty had not entered into force.

In situations where there is no DTA between your home country and Expatland, then great care needs to be taken if different family members reside in your home country, such as your wife and children.

A frequent misconception, especially between countries such as Australia and Hong Kong, is that a working partner can be based in Hong Kong while their family reside in Australia, and the Hong Kong income is not taxable in Australia.

That is not the starting position to begin from. More often than not the working partner will want to travel home regularly to be with the family. In that eventuality, the expat is likely to be an Australian tax resident.

Given there is no double taxation treaty between Hong Kong and Australia (the China/Australia DTA does not apply) prima facie; Australia has the right to tax the foreign income.

While we are not providing specific advice, we wish to draw your attention to the importance of understanding if DTAs are in place and what they may have to say about residency.

Expatland Pensions

The treatment of pensions is also commonly dealt with under DTAs. A foreign pension or annuity distribution is a payment from a pension plan or retirement annuity received from a source outside your home country.

You might receive it from one of the following:

- Foreign employer
- Trust established by a foreign employer
- Foreign government or one of its agencies (including a foreign social security pension)
- Foreign insurance company
- Foreign trust or other foreign entity designated to pay the annuity.

Similar to your home country pensions, usually the taxable amount is the gross distribution minus the cost (investment in the contract). Depending upon your location in Expatland, income received from such foreign pensions or annuities may be fully or partly taxable.

Many expats will, at some stage, begin accruing pension benefits because their foreign employer is required to contribute to a company scheme or a national scheme (such as the CPF scheme in Singapore). Other expats may begin receiving pensions from their home country if they remain in Expatland at or after retirement.

As a general rule, the pension/annuity articles of most DTAs allow the country of residence (as determined by the residency article) to tax the pension or annuity under its domestic laws. This is true unless a treaty provision specifically amends that treatment. As a general rule, the pension/annuity articles of most DTAs allow the country of residence (as determined by the residency article) to tax the pension or annuity under its domestic laws – for example, the UK/New Zealand Double Tax Agreement. This is true unless a treaty provision specifically amends that treatment. For example, consider the Belgium/Hong Kong Double Tax Agreement that allocates the tax right to the former country of residence.

There also may be special rules for lump-sum distributions. You need to look at each DTA carefully.

In the case of government pensions, generally speaking a DTA will protect a person in receipt of a state pension from their home country. The relevant DTA does this allocation to confirm which country you will pay tax to while you are receiving the pension.

In certain cases, some expats may also be subject to a double contribution agreement, which allows a company to send a worker to another country for a period of time but continue to pay the taxes and social security contributions of the home country.

Occasionally the government in Expatland may refuse to uphold the treaty claim. In this case you will need to make a treaty claim in your income tax return or by some other manner and file it with the foreign country. If tax was withheld it should be the case that you can claim a foreign tax credit.

Foreign Social Security Pensions

Most DTAs also have rules covering social security payments. Generally foreign social security payments are taxed by the country that makes the payments.

If the DTA is silent on the subject, then the usual case is that foreign social security pensions are taxable as if they were foreign pensions or foreign annuities.

Unless a specific DTA allows it (for example, the US/Canada Double Tax Agreement), they are not eligible for exclusion from taxable income the way a US Social security pension might be.

Social Security

As noted earlier, some parts of Expatland have a social security system and you can be required to contribute to it. Furthermore, you may also be required to take out private medical insurance as a condition of entry. (See Appendix C, 'Key Questions for Health Insurance Providers & Websites', for help with finding health insurance providers in Expatland.) It is therefore important to recognise and plan for these costs.

One of the benefits of these types of countries where you may be required to contribute to the social security system is that you can also receive government benefits such as access to healthcare and/or family allowances.

This is the case with EU nationals who are expats and moving from one part of the EU to another part of the EU. These expats are eligible for benefits in the arrival country after they have paid sufficient contributions in their country of origin (although there are currently restrictions applying to the new Eastern European EU countries and their nationals).

Many countries have bilateral social security agreements between them with the effect that social security contributions made in one part of Expatland can count towards pensions or other benefits in your home country.

Expat Tax Incentives

Given the global competition for expats, some of the countries in Expatland offer reduced tax rates or exempt offshore income of expats from taxation for a certain period of time.

A number of countries – for example Japan, Denmark, China, to name a few – vary the basis of taxation that applies to expats when compared to citizens of their own countries. This type of favoured treatment recognises the practical realities of the need to attract talent to a particular market.

You need to be aware of some of these benefits prior to making a decision to favour one part of Expatland over the other. For example, most expats going to the Middle East are attracted by the zero tax rates on offer.

These tax savings offer compensating adjustments for other inconveniences or difficulties in some locations.

Other parts of Expatland allow expats to only pay tax on that part of their salary that they derive from within the country; dual contracts or split contracts can also be an effective technique to manage your tax burden in certain countries.

Capital Gains Tax

Many parts of Expatland have some form of capital gains tax when you buy and sell assets. Real estate, for instance, is a common form of asset that is routinely exposed to capital gains tax.

You need to take care in understanding how capital gains tax might apply on future sales of any assets you left behind in your home country in Expatland.

Foreign Employer Pensions & Personal Contributions to Your Pension

If you worked abroad, in some parts of Expatland the cost of your pension might include amounts contributed by your employer that were not included in your gross income.

Additionally your contributions made while you were in your home country may not be treated as income either.

AT A GLANCE

- It is essential that you consider all the tax implications in your Expatland before you head off; six months is the preferred length of time to plan even if you are heading to a no-tax jurisdiction.
- In getting taxation advice, make sure you use a company who has specialist experience and will focus on you, not your employer.
- Plan for both tax perspectives from the point of view of your home country and also your Expatland, otherwise thousands of dollars could be added to your global tax bill.
- Find out if your home country has an exit tax regime. For example, Australia and the US have an exit tax regime.
- Be aware that other taxes can reduce your wealth apart from income tax, such as property tax, wealth tax and/or estate taxes.
- Some parts of Expatland have social security systems that you may be required to contribute to. Research this carefully before you leave.
- Don't let a tax decision drive a financial decision.
- Examine the implications of double tax agreements (DTAs) carefully.
- Don't assume that the tax treatment of an income stream in your home country will be the same in Expatland.

- If you are able to use the tax services of a Big 4 firm paid for by your employer don't forget to ask about the consequences of leaving your home country as well as the tax consequences of arriving in Expatland.
- Keep your income tax records as the Income Tax Authority in Expatland may request these for the purpose of calculating your tax position in Expatland.

14

EXPATLAND RETIREMENT

One of the key groups moving to Expatland are retirees who, having worked and completed a career in their home country, are motivated to move and live overseas.

As with most things in life, planning is the key.

First conduct a review of the Expatland countries that appeal to you. Some of the following key tips will help in your research:

1. General cost of living and trends over the past 10 years

2. Healthcare and costs of obtaining health services

3. Domestic travel costs

4. International travel costs including to and from your home country

5. Infrastructure and Information Technology availability

6. Banking services

7. Social customs and emerging trends

8. Access to social security from your home country if available

9. Key features of the taxation system

10. Understanding the tax consequences of leaving your home country.

It is wise to also remember that with more time in retirement, living expenses generally rise.

If you have dependents when you retire, then you need to consider the costs and impact of repatriating funds to those dependents.

Costs may rise for many reasons – including costs of bank transfers to funding airline tickets for dependents to visit you. You will also need to consider what level of support your dependents may require.

As previously noted, the income tax rate in Expatland will have a material impact on your after-tax income.

It makes sense to consider the level of income you wish to have in retirement and then using appropriate software to model what is the likely level of retirement capital you will need. Using the services of a financial planner or private banker is a sound strategy to make sure you are covering all the areas you need to.

State Pensions

If you have social security contributions in your country of origin, you may be entitled to a pension when you retire. However, be aware that although the retirement age in Expatland may be lower than your home country, you will not generally be able to claim a pension until you reach the retirement age of your home country.

The amount to which you are entitled will vary from home country to home country. You should start exploring your pension options as soon as possible upon arrival in Expatland.

Most countries have a defined level of contributions that must be made before you are entitled to claim a state pension.

Find out if you can contribute to a home country pension scheme while you are in Expatland. This may allow you to add to your eventual pension entitlements. Indeed, some countries will pay your pension into a foreign bank account.

If this is not the case, then you will need to have it paid into your home country bank account before it is forwarded to you in Expatland. However, this will probably lead to higher bank charges.

As a result, it is worth remembering that the sooner you start planning for your retirement the better. It is therefore imperative to begin your pension and retirement planning as soon as you arrive in Expatland.

In some parts of Expatland it may be possible to secure a state pension if you attain permanent residency. Some countries allow this but many impose limitations – for example, states in the Gulf.

Personal Pension Plans

For those who have a private pension scheme, this is usually arranged in conjunction with the employer whereby both the employee and the employer can make contributions.

When you leave your employer to join another, frequently you will have superannuation balances built up in various locations. Take care to track and monitor the various locations in which superannuation balances may have built up.

Similar to government pensions, claiming your money directly from your home country government when you have retired abroad can have an added level of complexity to it.

There are usually a number of payment options as to how the money is spent. Most pension providers will allow members to withdraw money as a lump sum, a monthly or annual payment or sometimes a combination of the two.

When considering which option is suitable for you, there are a number of factors to consider including tax implications and your living requirements. It is therefore advisable to take professional advice.

It is worth noting that recent changes in EU regulations ensure that EU citizens who move countries are still allowed to make contributions and receive payments if they are in one of the other EU member states. The reason for this is to facilitate free movement of people among trans-Europe employers.

AT A GLANCE

- Remember that with more time in retirement living expenses generally rise. If you have dependents when you retire, consider the costs and impact of repatriating funds to those dependents.
- Start exploring your pension options as soon as possible upon arrival in Expatland.
- Think about how much income you wish to have in retirement. Use software to model what is the likely level of retirement capital you will need.
- Consult with a financial planner or private banker to make sure you are covering all the areas you need to.
- Take care to track and monitor the various locations in which your superannuation balances may have built up.
- Ensure that if you move through Expatland you record the location of your various pension plans and understand any rules relating to forfeiture of retirement or pension funds.
- Recent changes in EU regulations ensure that EU citizens who move countries are still allowed to make contributions and receive payments if they are in one of the other EU member states.

APPENDICES

Appendix A

Special Terms

Active income: Income for which services have been performed. This includes wages, tips, salaries, commissions and income from businesses in which there is material participation.

Appointor (in a trust): The appointor or protector is the person or persons who have the authority under the trust deed to appoint or remove the trustee of the trust. As such the appointor is often said to be the controller of the trust. Many trust deeds empower the appointor to remove the trustee and appoint a new trustee at any time in writing. Unless specified in the trust deed or in the Will of the appointor, on the death of the appointor, the legal personal representative of the deceased appointor will become the appointor.

Arm's length transaction: 'Arm's length transaction' means a transaction where the parties to the transaction are dealing with each other at arm's length in relation to the transaction.

Business succession plan: A business succession plan is a document that outlines the proposed steps that will follow a change in the directors and/or shareholders of a business following the retirement, illness or premature death of the operators of the business.

Capital: Capital is different from money. Money is used simply to purchase goods and services for consumption. Capital is more durable and is used to generate wealth through investment. Examples of capital include plant and equipment, patents, software and brand names. All of these things are inputs that can be used to create wealth. Besides being used in production, capital can be rented out for a monthly or annual fee to create wealth.

Capital beneficiaries: These are beneficiaries who are entitled to the corpus of the trust or the capital in the trust. This entitlement does not usually arise until vesting day, or the day the trust is to be wound up, but entitlements to capital or corpus of the trust may occur earlier if permitted by the trust deed or agreed to by all beneficiaries.

Capital gains tax: A capital gain or capital loss is the difference between what it cost you to acquire an asset and what you received when you disposed of it. You pay tax on your capital gains. In some countries it forms part of your income tax and is not considered a separate tax, although it is generally referred to as capital gains tax.

Civil law: The civil law system derives from Rome. It is a body of law that sets out private rights and remedies, and regulates disputes between individuals in such areas as contracts, property and family law. Civil law comprises a body of doctrines compiled by legal professionals over many years. These doctrines have been used by legislators and administrators in civil law countries to form the basis of a code by which all legal disputes are decided.

Common law: The common law system, as developed in the UK, forms the basis of many legal systems. It is distinct from the civil law systems that operate in Europe, South America and Japan, which are derived from Roman law. Other countries that employ variations of the common law system are the US, Canada, New Zealand, Malaysia and India.

Community property law: Community property refers to the rules that apply to marital property. The law originated from civil law countries. It has extended in its application to common law countries. Generally speaking, in countries applying community property laws, property acquired after the marriage (excluding from inheritances or gifts) is treated as jointly owned. Then upon death, or divorce or annulment, the property is divided equally. Furthermore joint ownership is the presumption of the law in the absence of evidence to the contrary.

Controlled foreign corporations: Broadly, a controlled foreign company is a company that is not a resident of a certain jurisdiction but it is controlled from within the jurisdiction.

Default beneficiary: A default beneficiary is simply the beneficiary to whom a distribution may default to in the absence of any other nominated beneficiary in a trust.

Discretionary trust: A discretionary trust, which may also be known as a family trust, allows the trustee (who is usually the head of the family) to exercise discretion on an annual basis as to which beneficiaries will receive a distribution and to what extent each beneficiary shall benefit.

Dividend streaming: In general, dividend streaming refers to the practice whereby dividends are directed to benefit some shareholders at the exclusion of other shareholders. This is usually done so that credit for tax paid at the company level can flow to the preferred shareholder group.

Double contribution agreement: Generally speaking this refers to agreements between governments. They provide, among other things, that where a worker is sent on secondment from one country to the other, both the worker and the employer are liable to contribute only to the home country's scheme eliminating the liability to contribute simultaneously to the social security schemes of both countries.

Double taxation: Double taxation refers to the same income being taxed twice – usually by two federal governments. An example may be foreign earnings that are taxed where the work was carried out and also by the country of residence. One of the objectives of double taxation agreements is to prevent double taxation and allocate taxing rights to one government or the other.

Double taxation agreements: Generally a double taxation agreement is an agreement between two governments that regulates taxation matters concerning its citizens or corporations formed in their respective territories.

Dual contracts/split contracts: Dual or split contracts refers to the practice of an employee entering into two employment agreements on the basis that some employment duties are performed domestically for an employer and some duties are performed internationally for the same employer (or a related group company). The practice, most commonly used in countries like Hong Kong and until 2013 in the UK, was designed to assist the executive manage their personal income tax exposure.

Estate plan: An estate plan generally refers to the set of documents prepared in anticipation of the death of an individual. The usual objective of the estate plan is to meet the goals of the client and hence it may be relatively straightforward or quite complex.

Estate taxes: Estate taxes refer to the taxes that arise on the death of an individual. Many countries have estate taxes or 'death duties' as they are called in some countries.

Exit tax regime: This refers to a country that imposes taxation on citizens and/or other residents leaving its country to reside elsewhere. An example of this type of system can be seen in Australia, where the 'exit tax' requires the departing individual (it also can apply to other structures) to calculate the value of unrealised gains and losses and pay tax in the year of departure.

Foreign annuity: A foreign annuity is generally paid by a foreign party (for example, an insurance company) and it relates to a fixed sum of money that is payable each year for a defined term. It can be for the term of your life or for a set period. It is most commonly understood to relate to an investment product, but it can also be a benefit paid under a Will.

Foreign currency broker: A foreign currency broker is a person or entity that deals in buying and selling foreign currency.

Foreign pension: Similar to a foreign annuity, a foreign pension is the term used to describe payments received generally in respect of retirement from a pension plan.

Foreign tax credit: A foreign tax credit refers to the process whereby income tax paid overseas on foreign income is able to be utilised to reduce domestic tax otherwise payable.

Global taxation: 'Global' taxation (which is now quite unusual in developed countries) is a method whereby a country taxes profits of its residents wherever they are earned in the world.

Holding company: A holding company is usually described as the top company in a group structure. It holds shares in subsidiary companies in a corporate group.

Healthcare directive: A health directive is a formal way of giving instructions for your future healthcare and comes into effect only if you are unable to make your own decisions.

Hybrid legal system: A hybrid legal system refers to a legal system that utilises both common law and civil law in the administration of its justice system. An example of such a country with a hybrid legal system is Mauritius.

Hybrid trust: A hybrid trust is a combination between a discretionary trust and a unit trust. Some rights are fixed – for example, voting – and other rights are flexible, such as rights with respect to the receipt of income.

In specie distribution: In the context of a deceased estate an 'in specie' distribution is the manner in which beneficiaries under a Will receive the actual asset as opposed to the asset being sold and there being a distribution of cash.

Income: The amount of money earned from personal exertion and/or business or trade or from undertakings and investments.

International trust: A trust that is formed outside the country of residence of the beneficiaries and where at least one of the trustees is an international company.

JITSIC: JITSIC refers to the Joint International Tax Shelter Information Centre, which was established in April 2004 by the Commissioners of the Australian, Canadian, UK and US tax administrations.

Life-time gift: This term refers to the amount an individual is able to give away under certain tax regimes.

Living will: This term refers to a document that details a person's wishes in relation to their medical treatment in situations where they are no longer able to provide informed consent.

Maternity indemnity insurance: Commonly this refers to 'hospital indemnity' plans that cover maternity expenses.

Offshore financial centre: An offshore financial centre is the term used to describe a country or territory that has little or no income or capital gains taxes and minimal government interference in the regulation of business – for example, no requirement to lodge income tax returns or other reporting documents. It has a legal system that protects information from general public access and which provides advantages in particular industries such as insurance, banking, shipping and IP protection.

Passive income: Passive income includes certain types of dividend, interest, royalty, annuity and rental income. It is also includes gains on the disposal of assets that produce passive income or that are not used solely in carrying on a business.

Power of attorney: A document termed a power of attorney is a written authorisation to act on behalf of another person generally in the management of their private family business or in relation to certain transactions they wish to undertake. The authorising party is referred to as the 'donor'. The person authorised to act is referred to as the 'agent'. This role is usually granted to a trusted friend, professional advisor or family member.

Probate: In the context of this publication the 'probate' of a Will refers to the process of proving that the Will is genuine before a court. In some countries this court is the probate court. In common law countries a Will cannot generally operate until it has been admitted to probate. Hence it must be probated.

Revocable trust: The term refers to any trust, which can be revoked or cancelled upon the actions of the settlor of the trust.

Saving clause: In the context of double taxation agreements, a 'saving clause' ensures that each country to the double taxation agreement has the right to tax its own residents as if no double taxation agreement had been entered into. This has a certain amount of common sense to it in that no country will usually want to be restricted in its abilities to tax its own residents. There are exceptions to this and hence each double tax agreement has to be considered on its own merits.

Settlor (in a trust): The settlor is the person who brings the trust into being. Typically the settlor is a family friend or business associate who will contribute initial capital to settle the trust.

Tax haven: This term is used to describe those countries that do not impose any form of tax on income or capital.

Tax Information Exchange Agreement: Tax information exchange agreements (TIEAs) are important tools in assisting many governments combat offshore tax avoidance. Under TIEAs, it is usually the case that treaty partners must have legal and administrative frameworks available to support their commitment to exchange information.

Territorial taxation: Territorial taxation is based on the principle that a country taxes profits made in that country and leaves other countries to tax profits earned in their country.

Testamentary trust: A Will trust or a deceased estate arises on the death of a person. Upon death, property of the deceased passes to their estate. The fiduciary obligation to administer the estate and the assets therefore falls upon the executor or administrator who assumes the role of trustee in respect of the property of the deceased estate. The beneficiaries of a deceased are those nominated in the Will of the deceased.

Tiebreaker rules: The term 'tiebreaker rules' in a tax sense refers to the process whereby the residence of an individual or company is decided under a double tax agreement by reference to certain factors including but not limited to existence of a permanent place of abode, presence of family connections and a person's centre of vital interests.

Trustee: A trustee is the person who holds an interest in trust property for a committed trust object or purpose. In a discretionary trust situation the trustee exercises control over trust property so the trustee can deal with it on behalf of beneficiaries. The choice of a trustee is worth proper consideration for the reason that the trustee's powers and duties are significant. In that regard the person who is appointed to the position must understand their role and responsibilities. Trustees may be individuals but more commonly will be companies to limit liability. In a family trust a parent or both parents will usually act as directors of a corporate trustee.

Unit trust: Unit trusts are commonly used when arm's length parties wish to enter into a commercial undertaking together. Each party's entitlement to income and capital from the trust is proportionate to the units held.

Unvested shares: This term generally refers to shares issued by an employer entity to an employee that do not 'vest' until the occurrence of a certain event. Usually it is the effluxion of time or other key conditions that need to be met before the shares vest or become the property of the employee.

Vested shares: This term generally relates to shares issued by an employer to an employee that have become the property of the employee after certain conditions have been satisfied. The shares are said to have 'vested'.

Will trust: This is a trust created pursuant to a Will.

SOURCES: ATO website; cbi.org.uk; Investopedia; *Expatland*

Appendix B

Expat Views from Expatland

Hearing about experiences from expats in different countries can be useful in your own big move. Here are responses from some expats to a questionnaire we sent out. They give an overview of key points to consider when moving to Expatland. (The answers are representative of their feedback and have been edited for brevity.)

Q1: What were your expectations about expat life?

Answer 1: Significantly lower tax and a new adventure. I left my native Australia to eventually start my own venture abroad after having first established a good network.

Answer 2: I guess I was naïve, but I had no idea how hard it would be. However, my expectations that there would be greater opportunities were definitely met.

Answer 3: I left expecting to stay around 18 months; I've been here six years now.

Answer 4: We moved in quite a hurry, so I didn't really give the move that much thought. I was more excited than anything and focused on the 'big picture'– new places, new opportunities and new friends, financial opportunities and personal development.

Q2: What was the most difficult adjustment for you on the journey?

Answer 1: Understanding the differences in culture and language was tricky. Not having an understanding of my tax obligations in my home country was also a problem and I wanted to get this sorted immediately.

Answer 2: The most difficult was working out how to do the simple tasks, like paying bills, finding services like handymen or where to purchase particular items. Food shopping initially took forever, as I was completely unfamiliar with the brands.

Answer 3: The constantly changing landscape of expat friends was difficult to deal with. Also, where I moved to was a 24-hour flight from home, so that was arduous.

Answer 4: All the big stuff was easy, but after the excitement wore off, it was small things like trying to arrange credit that was very difficult. When you arrive, you have no credit history; my credit history was made worse by not knowing how the credit card system worked in my Expatland.

Q3: Who helped you with the logistics before you moved to Expatland?

Answer 1: My employer provided funds for the move (using an expat relocation agency paid for by my employer) and my taxation advisor ensured that I took the right steps in structuring myself from a taxation point of view prior to leaving home.

Answer 2: The company I was working for provided me with a relocation contact. She mostly helped us with the insurances, social security ID and driver's licence. The rest of the stuff we worked out ourselves.

Answer 3: Aside from an international moving company, we were on our own.

Answer 4: Friends who were from the country I was heading to helped me out a lot.

Q4: Did you buy insurance products while you were overseas, such as medical, health or life insurance?

Answer 1: I had medical insurance, but it can be tricky in Asia. It's advisable to get proper advice on this as well as on other insurances, as the Terms & Conditions can be different to what you may be accustomed to in your home country.

Answer 2: We all have insurances; where I moved to Expatland it was essential to have good private insurance. Fortunately the company provided medical insurance cover.

Answer 3: Buying insurance where I moved to is as standard as my home country. We were not able to find renter's insurance, so we used a Lloyds' product with our broker who is based in the UK.

Answer 4: It was difficult at first. Initially we had to use travel insurance and then we moved to temporary migrant insurance. Now a US company employs me, so it's easier.

Q5: Did you leave behind investments when you moved to Expatland?

Answer 1: I was moving to Singapore and my tax advisor told me I would be better off having assets and profits in Singapore. I did acquire assets after in Expatland, but I highly recommend that expats make sure they are properly advised about their taxation implications first up.

Answer 2: We did leave behind investments, but left securing these with our tax advisors. They gave me really valuable advice – and just the day before I flew out!

Answer 3: Being a young couple, our investments are pretty black & white with management done on our own.

Answer 4: I had small amounts of mutual funds in my children's names. I haven't had to do much in terms of managing them, but I can do so online if need be.

Q6: Has living in Expatland been a positive experience?

Answer 1: Wealth creation, career development, meeting international contacts and doing business on a far larger scale than in Australia have made it a positive experience for me. I intended staying two years, but it has now been 10 years.

Answer 2: Many professionals do not leverage the fantastic opportunity on their doorstep to have a better life abroad. They are unaware of all the significant benefits from a financial and personal view. I would advise people to do themselves a favour and look carefully at the benefits of moving to Expatland.

Answer 3: The friendships I've made and the business opportunities have been fabulous.

Answer 4: I loved expanding my horizons and meeting new people. I also love my career in Expatland; there wouldn't be much scope at home for what I do.

Q7: How do you manage your home country taxes while living in Expatland?

Answer 1: I have found it is best to keep the home country money as simple as possible. We don't use credit cards and all our expenses are on the one bank account. The family trust is also run through one account only.

Answer 2: Personally I have never found filing a tax return difficult; they are fairly standard from year to year.

Answer 3: It was easy, but it helps to know a few people.

Answer 4: I found it very difficult as I had properties and shares in a number of countries. It was very confusing adjusting to multiple tax systems.

Q8: How did you find a place to live?

Answer 1: An expat relocation agency (that my employer paid for).

Answer 2: We were very lucky to have friends who were agents, and they located a residence. I also visited a few months before the move as well to get a feel for the different areas and schools.

Answer 3: The company engaged our first real estate agent. In the end, it was an old friend who arranged our condo.

Answer 4: A friend drove us around and gave us the do's and don'ts. But because we didn't have any credit history in Expatland, we could only rent via craigslist [craigslist is a classified advertisements website with sections devoted to jobs, housing, personals, for sale, items wanted, services, community, gigs, résumés, and discussion forums].

Q9: How did you find schools for your children?

Answer 1: We first looked around the neighbourhood, then my wife spoke to her network as well as researched which of the schools would be best.

Answer 2: Checking out different suburbs gave me a feel for the type of people who lived there and attended the schools in the area. Then it was a matter of looking online to see which schools rated best.

Answer 3: I asked within my community for advice in this regard.

Answer 4: When you have kids, you are usually around people who have kids the same age. Everyone talks and shares information – you get to know the names of the schools then go and visit them. We made the decision based on the quality of the school and the proximity to where we lived.

Q10: What was the change in the cost of living when you moved to Expatland?

Answer 1: Having lived in Sydney, rental was similar, but the apartment was like living in a resort!

Answer 2: Meat and alcohol was expensive, but fruit and veggies were inexpensive.

Answer 3: Everything is cheaper by 50 per cent where I moved to. You can have an amazing lifestyle in my Expatland.

Answer 4: It all balanced out – some items were cheaper and others more expensive. Cars, fuel, clothes, liquor and food were cheaper, but rent was more expensive.

Q11: What advice would you give to a family about preparing the big move overseas?

Answer 1: Get a consensus from the family first and then take all the advice and help you can find. First-hand advice is always the best, and I also went online onto forums for some helpful tips.

Answer 2: Prepare for the move to cost you a lot more money than you think. In the first year, it is all a blur; in the second year, it can be tougher, and it will either prompt you to leave or make you decide to stay; in the third year, everything will be much easier.

Answer 3: It is also best to work on the minutia straightaway, such as organising your driver's licence, car, gas, phone and credit cards. If you move with the view that you are moving forever, that will make you integrate faster. Even if you change your mind later, at least you will be set up to stay if you decide to.

Answer 4: Be prepared for the fact that it will be exciting in the beginning, but then after a few years you will probably want to go home.

Q12: What has been the hardest thing for you living in Expatland?

Answer 1: At times communication and the cultural differences have been difficult. I've had to watch that my work/life balance has not been skewed towards too much work.

Answer 2: You also need to keep an eye on the higher level of discretionary spending capability that can lead to higher spending – the more you earn, the more you spend!

Answer 3: I miss family members and friends, the Mediterranean weather and the beaches. But airfares are so much cheaper now, so these issues aren't as significant.

Answer 4: The hardest thing for me was getting credit lines opened.

Q13: Did you make as much financial progress as you envisaged while living the expat life?

Answer 1: Yes, it allowed me to take more risks that were successful than if I were still in my home country.

Answer 2: It is still too early to say, but we didn't make the big move just for financial reasons – it was also about the experience.

Answer 3: I had to bear the brunt of the 2008 GFC, but still I think we are ahead of my peers back home.

Answer 4: Not yet, but we are slowly getting there.

Appendix C

Key Questions for Health Insurance Providers & Websites

1. Does the proposed plan provide for a cooling off or cancellation period with a full repayment of any premium?

2. What is the basis of the proposed plan – full underwriting or moratorium?

3. If the plan is a moratorium plan, for how long are pre-existing conditions excluded?

4. Is a medical examination required as part of the application process?

5. What customer service facilities support the proposed insurance plan? Is there a 24-hour customer service line, available from anywhere in the world, seven days a week?

6. Do restrictions apply to certain passport holders or for residents in certain country locations?

7. Is the plan guaranteed renewable or is it cancellable at the option of the insurance company?

8. Is there an excess before any claim can be paid out?

9. Please provide me with a projection of any increases over the next 10 years due to age.

10. Can I choose my own doctor or medical specialist or must I use a panel doctor?

11. Are there any conditions applicable before I seek medical help?

12. Do I have access to any hospital of my choice?

13. If I need medical attention, what is the bill payment and settlement process? Do the bills go direct to the insurance company?

14. Do I get cheaper cover if other family members join the plan?

15. What are the processes with respect to outpatient claims?

16. What is the normal period of time that claims are paid by?

17. What are the dispute resolution procedures in the event of a non-payment of a claim?

18. If I am travelling, what are the exclusions for my insurance cover?

Global Health Insurance Providers Websites

For more information on global healthcare providers, please visit the following:

1. https://www.allianzworldwidecare.com/international-individual-health-insurance?choice=en

2. www.bupa.com

3. https://www.medibroker.com/expert-advice/quote-request/

4. http://www.healthcareinternational.com/index.php

5. https://www.cignaglobal.com/

Appendix D

Foreign Legal Systems

The Australian Financial Review reported on 21 May 2013 that Australian businessmen Matthew Joyce and Angus Reed (former school friends) were convicted and fined $25m each in a bribery case. They faced the possibility of a decade in jail.

In May 2013, Joyce received the maximum sentence possible over a deal struck as part of a $40 billion development in Dubai in 2007. He had been detained in Dubai for four years prior.

Powerful dignitaries, such as the then Prime Minister Julia Gillard, then Foreign Minister Bob Carr, former prime minister Malcolm Fraser – and even the future King of England, Prince Charles, a fellow Geelong Grammarian – unsuccessfully lobbied on their behalf.

According to *The Australian Financial Review*, Australian courts conclusively documented their innocence, but the Dubai courts ignored revelations that the Dubai prosecutor and court had been misled.

Mr Joyce's Geelong Grammar school friend, Mr Reed, is based in Melbourne and faced possible extradition to the United Arab Emirates to serve 10 years in jail.

Another colleague, Mr Lee, who had also been detained in Dubai for close to five years, was acquitted of related charges. However, he lost all he had fighting the charges, including the family home, according to a report on the ABC, April 2014. Mr Lee was also unable to leave Dubai to attend the funerals of close family members during the legal wrangle.

As *The Australian Financial Review* reported, Mr Joyce was arrested after Gold Coast property developer Sunland alleged it was duped into paying a $12 million "introductory fee" to secure land on the Dubai waterfront at the height of the Emirates' property boom.

Sunland maintains that half of the introductory fee was transferred unbeknown to the company into a family trust account of Mr Joyce's in Jersey as part of a sham deal between Mr Joyce and Mr Reed.

However, in 2012 a Victorian Supreme Court dismissed Sunland's allegations and discredited as unreliable the evidence from Sunland founder Soheil Abedian and top executive David Brown.

The Dubai court ordered Mr Joyce and Mr Reed to repay the 44 million dirham "introductory fee" and pay a 44 million dirham fine, a total penalty equivalent to about $25 million each.

The recent ABC report stated that charges against both Joyce and Lee were finally thrown out and they were free to return to Australia.

Mr Reed had left the country before authorities struck, and was tried and convicted in absentia.

All three men have denied any wrongdoing in the deal Sunland has contended saw it pay $14 million for a non-existent right over the parcel of land known as D17.

Sources:

http://www.afr.com/p/national/property_duo_given_years_jail_in_eRqnCR WuECJqbcvjlwiAGI

http://www.abc.net.au/news/2014-04-08/marcus-lee-matt-joyce-dubai-\ corruption-falling-out/5373290

Appendix E

The Six Step Financial Planning List

The following steps will serve as a good guideline (based on the Investopedia.com website on financial planning):

1. **The Client/Planner**: The financial planner defines their responsibilities and yours. They outline how they will be remunerated for their services and who will remunerate them. As the client, you discuss and agree with the planner how long they will work for you and how the decisions concerning your finances will be made.

2. **Goals & Expectations**: Your financial planner will ask all the relevant questions about your finances, your goals (both financial and personal) and whether you prefer a high-risk or low-risk strategy, collecting all the relevant documentation.

3. **Analyses & Evaluation**: After gathering all the appropriate information, the financial planner will assess your information and determine the best course of action. This

could include examining your assets, liabilities and cash flow, current insurance coverage, investments or tax strategies.

4. **The Financial Plan**: Developing and presenting the financial planning recommendations and/or alternatives – the financial planner offers financial planning recommendations that address your goals, based on the information you have provided. The planner reviews the recommendations with you in order to help you make informed decisions. The planner listens to your concerns and revises recommendations as appropriate.

5. **Implementing the Recommendations**: You and the financial planner then agree on how recommendations will be carried out. The planner may carry out the recommendations for you or serve as a 'coach', co-ordinating the process with you and other professionals such as attorneys or stockbrokers.

6. **Monitoring the Plan:** You and your financial planner agree upon who will monitor your progress towards goals. If the planner is involved, they should report to you periodically to review the situation and adjust recommendations as needed.

Appendix F

Budget Template

See over page

Available for download on www.csttax.com

FAMILY CASH FLOW BUDGET FOR THE MONTH OF XX 20XX	MONTHLY BUDGET			ACTUAL			VARIANCE		
Date prepared:	Dad	Mum	Total	Dad	Mum	Total	Dad	Mum	Total
INCOME									
Net salary			$-			$-	$-	$-	$-
Net rent			$-			$-	$-	$-	$-
Interest			$-			$-	$-	$-	$-
Dividends			$-			$-	$-	$-	$-
Distributions from managed funds			$-			$-	$-	$-	$-
Other income			$-			$-	$-	$-	$-
TOTAL INCOME	$-	$-	$-	$-	$-	$-	$-	$-	$-
EXPENDITURE									
Accounting and tax fees			$-			$-	$-	$-	$-
Bank fees			$-			$-	$-	$-	$-
Council rates – main residence			$-			$-	$-	$-	$-
Donations			$-			$-	$-	$-	$-
Education			$-			$-	$-	$-	$-
Entertainment (Foxtel [cable TV], dinners etc.)			$-			$-	$-	$-	$-
Groceries			$-			$-	$	$-	$-
Home and contents insurance			$-			$-	$-	$-	$-
Income protection insurance			$-			$-	$-	$-	$-
Income tax (quarterly instalments and annual balance)			$-			$-	$-	$-	$-
Interest expense – main residence			$-			$-	$-	$-	$-
Legal expenses			$-			$-	$-	$-	$-
Life insurance			$-			$-	$-	$-	$-
Medical expenses			$-			$-	$-	$-	$-
Motor vehicle expenses (fuel, registration, R&M)			$-			$-	$-	$-	$-
Private health insurance			$-			$-	$-	$-	$-
Provision for living costs			$-			$-	$-	$-	$-
Repairs & maintenance – main residence			$-			$-	$-	$-	$-
Subscriptions (newspapers, magazines etc.)			$-			$-	$-	$-	$-
Superannuation – personal contributions			$-			$-	$-	$-	$-
Telephone – landline, mobile & Internet			$-			$-	$-	$-	$-
Travel & accommodation			$-			$-	$-	$-	$-
Utilities (electricity and gas) – main residence			$-			$-	$-	$-	$-
TOTAL EXPENSES	$-	$-	$-	$-	$-	$-	$-	$-	$-
NET SAVINGS FOR THE MONTH	$-	$-	$-	$-	$-	$-	$-	$-	$-